# Rabbit Keeping

Gav Nightingale

John Bartholomew & Son Limited

Edinburgh and London

British Library Cataloguing in Publication Data

Nightingale, Gay
Rabbit keeping - (Bartholomew pet series).
1. Rabbits
1. Title
636'.93'22    SF453

ISBN 0-7028-1099-1


*First published in Great Britain by*
JOHN BARTHOLOMEW & SON LIMITED
12 Duncan Street, Edinburgh, EH9 1TA and at
216 High Street, Bromley BR1 1PW


© 1979 John Bartholomew & Son Limited

ISBN 0 7028 1099 1




Printed in Great Britain
by Thomson Litho Ltd, East Kilbride, Scotland

# Contents

**CORRIGENDUM**

Page 72. The captions below the illustration on page 72 should read (from left to right); "Homozygous offspring, Heterozygous offspring, Homozygous offspring."

# General Care

A healthy, happy rabbit makes a much nicer pet than a neglected one, so daily attention is vital if your rabbit is to be fit and contented. Unfortunately for many pets, a keeper's experience comes slowly, and months or even years might pass before a full knowledge of the rabbit's requirements is gained. Naturally some people will have more success at first than others; some pet owners are more sympathetic to animal's needs than others, so learning to recognise a healthy rabbit is important.

**Buying the right rabbit**
Unless you have fallen for a beautiful bunny in your local pet shop, it is worth giving some thought to which breed you should buy. It is noticeable at large national shows that groups of people have a natural affinity with one breed rather than another. Some rabbit-keepers prefer the giant heavyweights, others go for miniature rabbits. Some like a big, fluffy bunny, while others favour a sleek greyhound type. Then there are fanciers who feel drawn to rabbits with long lop ears that sweep the floor either side of the head. Yet others want a pattern on their rabbit, or a very short, velvety coat. Or one particular colour might appeal, such as orange, blue or lilac. There is enough variety to keep everyone happy.

If you have found a little cross-bred rabbit in a pet shop, it might turn out to be docile. If you are still not quite sure which type of rabbit you like best, it could help if you consider the following points:

*Size:* This matters if you have limited space. There are pros and cons regarding the choice of large breeds or small breeds as pets. However, it cannot be stressed too strongly that if you have only a small hutch, or a limited area for hutches, then choose the Netherland Dwarf. It is true that the Polish is another tiny breed, but one difference is that the Polish is a sprightly animal requiring plenty of floor space, whereas the Dwarf is compact with a considerably less-arched body. The Dwarf needs exercise too, of course, but on the whole it will be more contented in the smaller

5

sized hutch than the Polish breed. However much the massive breeds attract you, think carefully whether you could provide the rabbits with the really long hutches that they require. The same rule should apply to the Belgian Hare — another sprightly *rabbit* that needs a six-feet-plus hutch.

Space available is not the only reason for considering size. It is well to remember that the heavier and larger rabbits will need proportionately greater quantities of food. Even a medium-sized rabbit will eat three to four times the amount of pellets and cereals that a Netherland Dwarf rabbit can manage. This point is best considered before you buy your first pet. If you are planning to feed lots of wild foods or home-grown greens, the economy factor may not matter so much. Or if you intend to keep only one pet rabbit, left-overs from the family table might form the major part of the diet, in which case a large breed could be chosen without an eye to food bills.

In order to gain some idea of adult size, it is best to note the ideal weight for each breed size, i.e. 2−2¼lb (1kg) is small; 6−8½lb (2kg) is medium-sized; 10−16lb (8kg) is large. All weights have been given in the Choice of Breed section.

Some would-be pet-owners might be wondering whether a large breed or a small breed makes the best pet for a child. Here there are varying opinions. It is generally thought that the Dwarf breed is suitable because it is light and, consequently, easy to handle. This is true — a larger breed can be awkward for a young child to pick up. Against this view, it is right to mention that most breeds can be managed by a sensible child of ten years or older, providing he or she has been properly taught from the beginning how to pick up a rabbit. Also, Dwarf rabbits tend to have rather an aloof manner. They seem very reserved and whereas one of the larger breeds might come eagerly forward to greet visitors, putting its feet up against the hutch door, the Dwarf is much more inclined to hold back. Because all rabbits have bones that could easily be broken with the wrong kind of handling, you need not fear that the Dwarf will be especially delicate. One point that I disagree with however is the claim that Dwarfs are more bad tempered than other breeds. In my experience, only strains of Dwarfs that have been in-bred for too long are bad tempered. Dwarfs that have not been too closely bred are quite docile and make gentle pets.

*Temperament:* This varies from animal to animal, just as personality does with people. A rabbit that has *always* been handled with extreme gentleness is much more likely to be docile than one that has been pulled about by unattended small children. Also, it has been noticed that rabbits kept without exercise in hutches that are too small, or rabbits repeatedly starved for two or more days, or rabbits kept without water for any length of time, are inclined to be vicious. Rabbits that are not often removed from their hutches with confident hands are likely to struggle and possibly scratch. This is due to a feeling of insecurity. Rabbits know when their owners are confident and they can sense when there is a chance that they could be dropped. Expertise in handling stock can only come with practice, and it does appear to be best if a child begins with a young rabbit.

*Age to buy:* If you remember that rabbits dislike change and show their disapproval by refusing to eat or act normally, you will appreciate that it is a good idea to purchase a young one. Most times if you buy mature stock, say over six months old, you buy trouble. However, unless you have had a lot of experience, do not be tempted to buy a very young rabbit, i.e. one less than seven or eight weeks old. This is especially important in the winter, for if you then acquire a rabbit as a pet, the sudden change from a warm hutch with brothers and sisters and the doe, to a cold hutch outside might be too great a shock for it. In the summer, when the nights are warm, even a beginner might successfully raise a young rabbit aged about six weeks upwards, but two extra weeks with the mother will give the youngster a better start.

If you decide to buy a pure-bred rabbit for breeding (preferably after having gained some previous experience with pet rabbits) go for a doe of about twelve weeks, as she will then have two or three months to settle down with you and your family environment before mating time draws near, at five to seven months for the small-to-medium breeds; seven months to a year for the large breeds.

*When to buy:* Spring is a good season to buy a young rabbit as a pet. Pleasant spring days, followed by warm summer and autumn, will allow plenty of time for learning about rabbit keeping. By the first dark days of winter, the new owner will have more knowledge and be better equipped to deal with the hazards of frost and icy winds. A regular feeding programme will have been arranged and turning out to make the rabbit comfortable for the night should be a matter of routine.

Obviously unless someone in the family is prepared to sacrifice a short amount of time every day for feeding, and a longer period once or twice a week for cleaning out the hutch, it is not the right moment to buy a pet rabbit. This is a point worth considering at the beginning, because a little rabbit in a pet shop window can look very appealing. It is difficult for many children (and parents!) to resist such temptation, but it is unfair to expect a child to take full responsibility at first. Many a rabbit has suffered when the children have lost interest after a few weeks. Unlike adults, they cannot remember to feed the pet every day until they have had a considerable period of watching a conscientious person attend to pets regularly. Responsibility is learnt. However much the child likes the pet and does not wish to harm it or cause distress by neglect, this can and will happen without the watchful eye of an adult. A little gentle reminding for the older child may be all that is necessary. However, it is a good plan to decide straight away who is going to be in charge of feeding, so that everyone in the family does not think that someone else is doing it! A rabbit is locked into its hutch and it cannot help itself. A cat will wander round the kitchen looking pathetic and even making a mewing sound when hungry, but so many rabbits have starved to death *in silence* within sight of green grass.

The care available at holiday times is worth considering too. Normally, it should not present any problems that are difficult to solve. Kindly neighbours often offer to attend to pets during the owner's absence. However, perhaps it would not be convenient to purchase a rabbit if you know you will shortly have to go on a long holiday abroad, or if your present commitments involve frequent family trips away from home.

*Doe or buck?:*   Several prospective owners have asked whether a doe makes a better pet than a buck or vice versa. In fact both buck and doe make excellent pets. The choice really depends on whether you have a natural feeling towards male or female animals in general (and funny though this may sound, some people appear to prefer one sex to the other in animals for quite obscure reasons). It will not be obvious when a doe is in season, and so unlike the female dog, she will not be a nuisance; and the buck will not become aggressive or difficult if he is deprived of access to does. He will stamp around and make attempts to escape if he is housed close to a doe's hutch; but this should not be a problem where a buck is kept on his own as a pet. Some people say that bucks make the best pets. This may be because a doe in a breeder's home is so often in kindle or feeding young, that she is better not handled by children, so the old buck becomes the well-loved family pet.

## How many?

The number of rabbits that you keep will depend on personal choice and the space available, but beware of over-crowding, because this can lead to miserable conditions, difficulties in cleaning out, and subsequent disease. All adult rabbits should have separate living quarters. A doe and a buck are never kept together permanently. Two does are occasionally housed in the same hutch if it is really large and spacious — not less than two square feet *per rabbit* for a small to medium-sized breed. Two bucks should never be kept together in the opinion of most. However, I have known three pairs of bucks, each of which had shared a hutch without mishap. It is important to realise that in all these cases the bucks had been together since babyhood and never known any other way of life. Bucks are inclined to fight, and if separated and then put together again after even a few days, fierce fighting will occur. Two strange bucks put into one hutch will almost certainly fight.

Two adult does will most likely fight if one is introduced to the other's hutch or wire exercise run. The fur will fly and biting and scratching will be in earnest — especially if one of the does is in kindle or with young.

Youngsters that have been recently weaned may be run on together in a large hutch or wire pen indoors until they are three months old. After this period, when the does will be separated from the bucks, each buck and each doe that you intend to keep should be given a separate hutch.

**Sexing**

It is surprising how many rabbit-owners do not know the sex of their pet. It can be difficult to distinguish baby bucks from baby does, but it is possible for the expert to sex at birth (though not advised), and the experienced rabbit-keeper has little trouble in deciding the difference when babies are two and a half weeks old. However, mistakes can be made even at six weeks by those with the know-how. You will have gathered that the young rabbit males and females look much alike, especially to the novice. There are signs that you can train yourself to recognize, and the best way to learn the correct technique is by watching an experienced rabbit-keeper sex a litter. The vent regions of does and bucks are similar until you press *very* gently on either side. The buck's organ will show as a minute rounded tip, and the doe's organ as a slit. Be warned: in the youngster, rounded tip and top of slit are extremely difficult for the beginner to tell apart. It might help if you observe the distance between the anus and the sexual organ in each case, as the penis of the buck is *slightly* further from the anus than the vulva from the anus in the doe.

Take care not to press the mature buck in this region. Not only is it entirely unnecessary, but you could easily cause pain. The adult male is readily distinguished from the female. If you carefully turn him over (supporting him properly so that he does not hurt his backbone) you will see two rather long testes (scrotal sacs) on either side of the vent area. Of course, the doe does not have these sacs. (See diagrams).

There are other differences between the buck and the doe, so the rabbit-fancier can often recognize a buck or a doe just by looking at the over-all appearance. Bucks usually have wide short heads, while the doe's head is slightly longer and more narrow. The baby doe is often larger than the baby buck — even the adult bucks are smaller than does of the same breed. However a sexual observation is the only way to be sure.

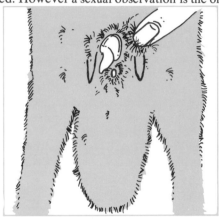

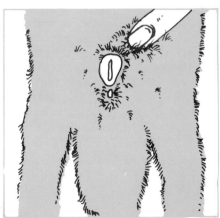

*Sexing young rabbits is difficult. The testes are not visible in the baby buck. In the early weeks the male and female sexual organs look similar, as they are undeveloped.*

**Where to buy**

Perhaps you have a friend who keep rabbits, or you know a rabbit breeder whose stock you can inspect to assure yourself that it is attractive and healthy. Otherwise, if you are sure which breed interests you most, your best method of obtaining a young rabbit is to contact the secretary of a specialist club. If you ask to be put in touch with a reliable breeder, who might have surplus stock to spare, you are sure to receive a helpful reply (see Useful Addresses). A third method is to buy from your local pet-shop, if it has a good name for selling healthy animals.

**The healthy rabbit**

It is useful to be able to tell by simple inspection if a rabbit is healthy or sick. You will need to know how to select a good youngster at the time of your original purchase, and how to spot an ailing animal as long as you keep rabbits. A sick rabbit needs treatment, culling, or isolation; and early action sometimes saves other stock from catching the same illness.

*A healthy rabbit*

The healthy rabbit has bright eyes, alert ears that twitch to catch the slightest sound, well-rounded muscles and a dry, clean area under the tail, but above all, look at the nose — there should be no discharge. Never buy a rabbit with signs of a running nose, no matter how wonderful it is in type or colour. If a youngster is hopping about with the rest of the litter that is as it should be. A lively animal is more likely to be healthier than one that sits huddled in one corner while the others jump up and down. A fluffed-up appearance with dull, half-closed eyes are warning signals in the rabbitry and with experience you can soon pick out the sick specimen. However, remember that youngsters of less than three or four weeks sleep for much of the day. This should not be mistaken for illness.

So a beginner should look for dry eyes, nose, and tail regions, and a generally alert appearance. In addition, if you are buying a rabbit of a particular breed, it is best to familiarize yourself with the Standard. There are set rules regarding exact colour shade, type of bone structure, density of coat, even pattern markings, etc., for each variety of every breed. It is essential to follow these rules if you intend to show. If you just want an attractive pet, one of a litter rather than a show rabbit would be suitable.

## What about a pedigree?

Pedigree in the rabbit world works in a slightly different way from the pedigree system employed in the cat and dog worlds. A pure-bred rabbit

*B.R.C. ring on hind leg*

of a recognized breed is given a British Rabbit Council leg ring by its owner. These are made of aluminium, which is an extremely light metal, and they do not seem to cause any more discomfort than, say, a wedding ring. They are sold in batches of five and the different breeds have special sizes which have letters according to the size of the rabbit. The letter follows the year the rings were purchased. For example, a Dutch rabbit rung in 1979 might be 79 B 10000. The correct ring (with the right letter for the breed) is pushed gently over the hock of a back leg when the rabbit is about six weeks old for small breeds, or eight weeks for a large breed. A week or two later it will be impossible to remove. It forms a permanent record of the rabbit. It is possible to tell approximately how old a rabbit is by glancing at the year number on the ring. If you sell a rabbit with a ring, a transfer card is sent to the British Rabbit Council and for a small fee the purchaser's name is registered as the new owner. These details become more important to anyone interested in showing their pets, as a rabbit that is not wearing a ring will not be accepted.

## Cost

Rabbit-owners are entitled to charge what they like for pure-bred stock, but it often happens that well-marked rabbits of excellent type change hands for no more than token payments. Obviously, if the breeder has a good strain bred from champions, you should expect to pay a little extra. Indeed, an animal of perfect type might be worth £50 or more, but hundreds of pure-bred rabbits are sold every week for very much less. Most likely, your local rabbit-breeder will be pleased to see his spare stock go for a few pounds or dollars to a kind home. Probably much the same as the nominal sum you would have to pay for a cross-bred youngster at the pet shop.

## Bringing the rabbit home

Make sure you take a basket or a box when you go to buy your new pet. A frightened animal that struggles and twists about in an effort to escape is capable of doing itself considerable harm. I remember a rabbit that was sent on a long journey by rail. It jumped up in fright when the box was lifted for the last stage of the journey and killed itself by knocking its head on the lid. This was an exceptional case, but it shows how timid rabbits are and how much care needs to be taken when transporting them for any reason. Rabbits can travel safely by rail in a stout box, so long as the lid is labelled 'LIVESTOCK' in large red letters. It might be necessary to send away for a rabbit if you have chosen a rare breed, but at least you can find out what time the train will be arriving at your nearest station and arrange to meet it. Try to reduce the time the rabbit is in the travelling box as much as possible, e.g. avoid leaving it overnight at a station.

When your pet arrives home, pop it straight into the hutch that you have prepared in advance. See that there is plenty of dry bedding, a supply of food (not too much on the first day), and a container of clean water. Then (and this is most important) leave the animal alone for a few hours to settle down quietly in its new home. This way it will get over the shock of changing its environment. The changes will probably be considerable — just think for a moment:  besides losing its mother, the young rabbit will have to adjust to new surroundings, different bedding, pots, bottles, even the light coming from another direction. There will be strange people and strange voices as well.

It is sensible to find out what the breeder has been giving the baby rabbit to eat and at what times. You can then try to provide the same food at about the same times during the first week, so that at least part of the pattern of the rabbit's life remains unaltered. Later, you can slowly change to your own preferred routine. At first give the new pet half of its usual type of food and half of whatever kind of food you wish to introduce. This method will also have the benefit of allowing the rabbit's digestive system time to adapt to the new diet.

*Travelling-box*

**Cleaning out the hutch**
It is best to make light work of hutch cleaning and the only way to do this is to clean out regularly. The more often you do the job, the easier i

14

becomes. I have tried various kinds of bedding over the years and the materials I use at present are newspaper and straw. In wooden hutches several layers of newspaper are laid over the floor and a generous covering of straw is placed on top of the paper to one side of the hutch. The feed-pot is situated in an area where there is no straw. The benefit of this system is that the paper can be changed every day for does with litters. The newspaper is simply picked up and the soiled area and droppings folded into the middle. The whole package is then deposited on the compost heap. Where there is no compost heap the droppings can be dug straight into the garden, or put into a polythene bag to be given to a gardening friend. Rabbits without young are usually cleaned out once or twice a week. I find that if the job is left longer than this, the newspaper begins to disintegrate, with the result that a trowel has to be used to clear the wet corner and the job takes much longer. Where newspaper is in short supply, other forms of bedding can be used.

### Litter for hutches

*Sawdust:* This is probably the most popular bedding material. It is usually scattered liberally all over the hutch floor, so that it forms a deep layer to absorb urine. Once a week the wet sawdust is removed with a scraper and replaced with a fresh supply. Some rabbit-keepers using this type of material like to clean just the dirty corner twice a week, giving the hutch a thorough clear-out less often. Others choose to use some straw or hay in the sleeping compartment in addition to the sawdust.

*Wood shavings:* In some ways this material can be better than sawdust as there is less chance of the dust irritating the eyes, or getting into food and water pots.

*Dry peat:* This is widely used in areas where it can easily (and cheaply) be obtained. Peat soaks up moisture in a similar way to sawdust.

*Fallen leaves:* These are sometimes used at the time of year when they can be freely gathered. Rabbits not only like to eat dry leaves from fruit trees but also seem to enjoy having them around. Make sure they are not wet or mouldy.

*Hay:* This can be employed as bedding, but it is really a food for rabbits. It is rather a waste to spread good quality hay as bedding, and poor quality hay is usually unsuitable because the dust gets into the noses of the rabbits and can cause illness. However, stock that is housed outside will need some form of warm bedding and if hay is the only material available, then it must be used. If you do use it, make sure that you top it up regularly as your pet is capable of eating it all in the day time, leaving nothing for a bitterly cold night. If the weather seems to be getting colder, suspect a sharp frost and give even more bedding than usual.

*Equipment: bin, bucket, food dish, and scrapers*

*Straw:* One of the best forms of litter, it is cheap and readily available in most countries where rabbits are likely to be kept as pets. It is worth noting that it is not economical to purchase bedding materials for rabbits in small quantities. Tiny bags full of hay or straw do not go very far and they will most probably be expensive for the small amounts they contain.

If you can go to a farm and buy a bale, this may seem costly at the time, but it will work out much cheaper in the long run. However, you will need somewhere to store the bale. If you live in a town, you might have a garden shed or part of a garage where there would be enough space, but if you live in a flat (with just space for bunny outside), I agree that bedding in bulk can be a problem. Nevertheless, if it is possible, it is best to buy hay or straw by the bale, and always try to choose a good grade. A final word on cleaning out: although greens are much enjoyed by stock, greens do make a difference to hutch cleaning and to some extent to smell. This is especially noticeable when large quantities of cabbage or kale are fed. Whichever type of litter is used, when the bedding becomes wet it must be changed. Damp conditions are more dangerous than cold where rabbits are concerned.

*Doe with young in nest-box. The dark end of the hutch is boarded over in front, but this litter has been moved into the light*

*Young bucks and does should be separated at 10 weeks*

*Harlequin* Champion Weldman Lady Suzette *owned by Keith Bee*

*Best Orange Rex, Bradford 1979, owned by Mr. and Mrs. J.H. Phillips*

Sparky—*a Silver Grey buck owned by Mrs. Barbara Measey*

*Chinchilla Netherland Dwarf owned by K. Hopkinson*

*Dwarf Lop owned by Mr. and Mrs. J. Blundy*

*Black Silver Fox—Best of Breed at Bradford 1979 owned by Trixie Cuthbert*

*Californian*

*Himalayan Dwarf*

*How to hold a rabbit correctly:   take the weight with one hand and place the other hand gently over the ears. Never pick a rabbit up by its ears.*

### Handling

Pick your rabbit up carefully every time and you will have a good-tempered animal for a pet. Frequent handling will not do any harm so long as the lifting is skilful. With the exception of a doe in kindle or a very young baby in the nest, the more you take bunny out of his hutch the tamer he will become. You should always handle gently and firmly. From the moment you open the hutch door, your movements must be slow and quiet. Rabbits react in fear to jerky movements and sudden noise. They are not very clever in human terms, but they tend to remember rough handling. A rabbit that has been badly treated (even unintentionally) will cower at the back of its hutch when the door is opened, and remain there until left alone again. It is difficult to regain the confidence of such a pet once it has been lost, although a person with a lot of empathy with animals might succeed. Unfortunately, spitefulness is often the result of maltreatment of one kind or another. Children can be rough or noisy without realising that they are frightening their pets. This is a great pity as a rabbit responds to correct management by coming forward to greet its owner and by sitting quietly without struggling or scratching when held.

Teaching children to hold a rabbit the right way is helpful. A rabbit is *never* picked up by the ears alone — even for a few seconds. This is cruel. A rabbit is not picked up by the scruff of its neck. Many breeders do control a rabbit with one hand on the ears, but the other hand is *always* under the body to take the full weight. The hand on the ears is only to steady and calm the animal. The easiest way for a child to hold a rabbit is to place one hand under the rump and the other around the head and ears. The rabbit's body is held against the chest of the child. Someone should stand by to stop the child from pressing the rabbit's head too firmly the first time, as the natural grasp of anxious youth is too tight.

## Talking to rabbits

This is not so strange as it might sound. If you chat to your pets, while you are filling the food and water pots, they will come to know you and not be afraid of your voice.

Rabbits are normally silent animals, but they do make various sounds on occasions. They scream when they are terribly afraid, say, in the presence of one of their natural enemies such as a ferret, a dog, or even a larger and stronger rabbit. Otherwise, apart from the buck's cry after mating, a rabbit's cry is reserved for times when it feels extreme pain. Only the observant will hear the other little sounds they make. They murmur in a voice hardly audible to human ears. The sound is like a cross between soft grunts, heavy breathing, and a kind of broken purr. Baby rabbits talk to their mothers with these sounds. Adults do not 'talk' unless happy or highly excited.

Rabbits thump their back legs to talk to each other at a distance. If one rabbit thumps, all the others will stop eating or running about and freeze, as this is one of their danger signals. Sometimes one thump is answered by a thump from another rabbit.

There are other ways in which rabbits try to let people know their needs. One will turn his feed-pot upside down when it is empty; another will put his nose repeatedly in and out of an *empty* water-pot to show that he is thirsty. However, rabbits are not very intelligent and a few might think of these things, whereas many might not. Therefore, we should try to keep the water-pots full at all times. Rabbits do not learn tricks as easily as cats and dogs do, although they can be taught to sit nicely on the show bench by a patient and kind owner.

### Biting and scratching
Rabbits become vicious for various reasons; these include rough handling, starvation, cramped hutch space with little exercise, too many children poking and shouting (as in the case of a school pet). If your pet bites every time it is picked up, perhaps the kindest thing is to have it put down, but before taking this drastic step, consider the following exceptions: A doe with young might become temporarily snappy in order to protect her young — this is quite normal. Sometimes a pet bunny will look as though it is going to bite, even perhaps going so far as to take a piece of cloth into its mouth, but the teeth never sink in — this is a nervous gesture and common to many rabbits. A young doe in particular might bite nervously at her own dewlap (pouch of skin and fur under the chin) — it is just an instinctive reaction.

Scratching is usually the result of careless handling and rarely intentional. A rabbit will claw another rabbit when fighting, but will almost never scratch a human on purpose. Sometimes a claw will scrape the hand as a pet struggles for a secure foothold when picked up by a child.

### Mercy killing
It may seem awful to consider killing in a pet book, but it is something that every rabbit-owner should know how to do in case of emergency. Even if you feel you yourself could never kill, it might be helpful to be able to tell someone else how it is done quickly and painlessly. If a pet has a bad accident this is often the kindest thing to do. Breaking the neck causes instant death and is recognised as the most effective method. The neck is dislocated with a sharp backward jerk of the head. A thumb is placed behind the ears and while the hand pulls the head up at the front, the back of the head is pushed down. When it is done by an expert, the back legs are held in the other hand and the whole operation is done in one swift movement. If this method seems unsuitable for any reason, a rabbit can also be killed by a blow to the back of the head at the base of the skull. If both these methods are impossible, your local vet or People's Dispensary for Sick Animals will put your pet down with an overdose of anaesthetic.

### Management of moult
Your pet will shed its coat and grow a new one every year. This is a gradual process. A few hairs drop out at a time, although the fall is heavy

enough to show as a moult line on the coat. On one side of the body the new fur is thick and dense, while on the other side (lower down the body rather than lengthways) the fur is thin and 'moulty'. The nose and rump are the most usual places where the moult line can be seen clearly. Some rabbits take longer to get right through the moult than others.

The first fur that grows is known as the baby coat. At four to six weeks the intermediate coat begins to grow, and at four to five months the adult coat starts into its prime and is fully mature around six to nine months.

Many breeders will not mate their rabbits when they are in very moulty condition, for growing a new coat tends to take a lot out of a rabbit, so because a doe should be in good health for raising a litter it is well to mate when the doe has a full coat. However, if a mother had a thin coat at the time of mating, this does not mean that her babies will be born with poor coats and fur potential.

Some rabbits have been known to lick quantities of loose hair from their bodies during the moult and as a result have gone off their food. Apparently, the hair has blocked their alimentary canals for a short time.

An old pet, say seven to ten years or more, will most likely become rather lazy about washing and consequently become somewhat dirty in appearance, but a rabbit should not be bathed, as the fur is extremely dense and takes a long time to dry. If by chance a pet is left out in a wire run during a sudden shower of rain, it can be dried quickly with a hand-held hair-dryer. Take care to keep the temperature cool. Test it frequently by passing a hand in front of the warm air, while holding the dryer at a safe distance from the fur. Beware of burning!

**Manure**

A useful by-product of rabbit-keeping is the manure. Rabbit droppings plus urine-soaked hay or straw can be safely rotted down on the compost heap to make a most valuable vegetable fertilizer. There are few natural fertilizers that can equal rabbit manure. It is an excellent source of plant food, usually considered better than horse, cow, sheep or poultry manure.

Try to construct your compost heap on a large scale, rather than just filling a small tub or box. You will find it much easier to manage and the straw will rot down properly, turning into a fine, crumbly texture — just right for the garden. See how your flowers and vegetables will flourish once you keep rabbits!

After about three months, you might like to turn your heap sides to middle, preferably by forking it over onto an adjacent patch. This will ensure that the dry straw on the outside of the heap has a chance to rot to the same consistency as the straw on the inside. When all has rotted down, it should be a dark brown colour and crumble readily in your hand. There should be no unwanted smell, only a pleasant scent. Although fresh rabbit manure has a slight odour — not altogether unpleasant when the animals are healthy — it is not a good idea to build a compost heap of any kind too close to the house. Choose a site at the bottom of the garden if possible.

## Management of the Angora

The Angora has a section here as well as in the following chapter, because it requires exceptional care and attention.

One of the joys of keeping the Angora breed is that you can wear a coat made from the wool without killing the animal. The wool can be clipped every three weeks without harming the rabbit in the slightest way. You can continue these regular clippings throughout the rabbit's life, say for eight or more years.

There was a time when Angora wool was purchased from rabbit-keepers by industrial concerns in England. Nowadays there is no commercial outlet in Britain for home-produced Angora wool, but there has been a revival in hand-spinning.

Many Angora-breeders are using a simple wooden spindle in much the same way as it was used hundreds of years ago. There is something satisfying in breeding your own Angora rabbits, harvesting your own wool, then spinning and knitting it up into garments for your family. For the enthusiast it does not end there, because there is the fun of gathering herbs to make dyes for your wool, and possibly the excitement of graduating to a spinning wheel.

## Your Angora rabbit

When the time comes to buy a baby Angora, try to visit the breeder when a litter for sale is about eight weeks old. Look for the youngster that has non-matting wool behind the ears, as this will be the good one for wool production or showing.

You will need to take the young rabbit out of his hutch every day to get him used to being groomed, although you will not be using the wool for spinning until the youngster is around five or six months old, as garments made from the baby coat do not wash or wear well. By the time a rabbit is ready for clipping, it will be quite familiar with the grooming routine and will sit still. With a pair of hair-dresser's scissors and a great deal of care, you clip from just above the tail up to the neck in neat rows until the clipping is complete on the back. The wool on the lower side of the doe is usually left unclipped, as she will need this for lining her nest when her young are born. It is possible to obtain approximately 8 or 9oz (225–255g) of wool per rabbit in a year. Special attention should be given to avoid poking the delicate skin or the eyes. Sometimes a rabbit will turn suddenly and so it is a tricky job, but with practice is takes about half an hour to clip a rabbit.

## Show Angoras

The white Angora is the most popular colour at present, but there are twelve colours: blue, blue-cream, cream, blue-grey, brown-grey, chinchilla, chocolate, cinnamon, golden fawn, sable, smoke, and sooty-fawn. Wool on a show specimen might measure six inches (15cm) in length. White patches of wool in a coloured coat are frowned upon by judges, with the exception of the Agouti shades, when white on the underside of the tail is allowed.

It is essential to realise that Angoras will require more of your time than other breeds. You will need a lot of patience to keep up the daily grooming that is necessary in addition to the other routine tasks of feeding and cleaning. This is a lovely breed, but not the right one to choose if the time you have available for pets is limited.

Show Angoras are usually kept on wire floors to prevent the wool from becoming stained and matted. The wire floor is slipped in on a frame which exactly fits the floor of a wooden hutch. The recommended wire is ½in (12mm) mesh, which makes a firmer base than ordinary wire-netting. It does not sag, which is important for the rabbits' comfort. Rabbits kept purely as pets or for breeding may be housed in normal hutches on straw.

Anyone interested in self-sufficiency will want to colour their own wool with natural dyes. This is a fascinating subject, as many wild plants can be boiled, and when they are mixed with wool a wide range of subtle colours is obtained. A chemical substance often has to be used first to make the colour 'take' on the wool, for example, salt. The chemical is called a mordant. By changing the mordant, the same plant dyes will give different colours and shades.

# Choice of Breed

### Alaska
A thick-set, rounded animal with well-furred ears. This breed originated in Germany from crossings between Himalayan, Argente and Dutch rabbits. Brownish-black eyes and black nails are in keeping with the brilliant black colour of the coat. It is kept as a meat breed as well as for pets. A good specimen weighs between 7½ – 8½lb (3.4 – 3.8kg).

### American Giant
Black or blue marks on white with dark ears and a butterfly smut pattern on the nose distinguish this large breed. Toe-nails are white. What a beautiful animal for anyone that has space for a generous-sized hutch! Required weight: 11 – 12lb (5 – 5.5kg).

### Angora
There are two different types of this attractive rabbit. The English type has a fine, long, silky coat. The French Angora is a larger animal, producing more wool, but of a slightly coarser texture.

This is a breed to choose if you have plenty of time to spare, as the show coat needs grooming every day to prevent matting. The wool is blown, rather than brushed, into a complete ball shape without a tangle to be seen from head to tail. A first-prize winner is a breath-taking sight. Indeed, many Angoras have won Best in Show awards. British colours include: blue, chocolate, cream, golden fawn, chinchilla (see also Management of the Angora, p.21). Eyes can be blue, brown or red, according to the colour of coat. Weight: 6lb (2.7kg).

### Argente
An elegant French breed seen in four recognised colours: bleu, brun, champagne and crème. Rather oddly perhaps, the different colours have developed their own shape standards and the ideal weight also varies with the colour.

*Argente Bleu:*   This variety has a cobby, compact body. The undercolour is lavender, tipped with blue-white. (Blue guard hairs). Weight:   6lb (2.7kg).

*Argente Brun:*   A neat body as in the Bleu, only with the silver topping brown instead of blue. (Dark brown guard hairs). Weight:   6lb (2.7kg).

*Argente de Champagne:*   The oldest of the four varieties. The standard requires a body that is neither racy or cobby. A slate-blue undercolour is tipped with silver. It is interesting that the silvering appears only with the first moult. The general effect on an older rabbit is silver-white sprinkled with black hairs. In many breeds it is difficult to judge very young rabbits, as their true potential only becomes apparent as they mature. Dark ears are a fault in this breed, although the nose area may be of a darker shade than the body. Weight:   8lb (3.6kg).

*Argente Crème:*   Here we have the smallest one of the four, but still it must not be too cobby. The colour is orange under creamy-white with longer orange guard hairs. Weight:   5lb (2.3kg).

## Belgian Hare

This is a fascinating breed. Many people who are little acquainted with the rabbit world imagine this must be a kind of hare. They think that it must be a direct descendant from one of the wild hares. In fact this is not the case at all. It is a fancy breed of *rabbit* resulting from cross-breeding domesticated animals in a way similar to any of the other breeds. It was the colouring that led to the name 'Hare' being given to a rabbit. In the beginning, in Belgium, where it originated, it was a sandy-black colour. Now, the show specimen is long and lean with a bold hazel eye. The modern shade is a much richer chestnut than the wild colour.

It is often said that Belgian Hares make good pets, but it must be stressed that this is not a rabbit for a small cage. Long limbs should have exercise and a very roomy hutch. It would be cruel indeed to keep such a racy creature in a space where it could only just turn round. Weight:   8−9lb (3.6−4.1kg).

## Beveren

This rabbit has a luxurious fur coat that has to be seen to be believed. The blue is the oldest variety, but colours can now be blue, white, black or brown. The white is unusual in that it has blue eyes, as many white rabbits are albinos with pink eyes. In addition to their lovely coats, good points are the rather beautiful Roman-shaped nose and well-furred strong ears. This is a large breed. Weight: 8lb upwards (3.6kg−).

## Blanc de Bouscat

Another large breed, but all white and like the rabbit in *Alice in Wonderland:* long, wide ears, domed head, pointed nose, well-rounded body, smooth coat. In spite of the large size, the bones are fine. It was bred in 1906 in France and is mainly kept in rabbitries for meat and fur. There is now a specialist breed club in the United Kingdom for those interested in showing this rabbit or keeping a buck or doe as a pet. Weight: 13−15½lb (6−7.1kg).

## Blanc de Hotot

A French white rabbit, not very well known in the United Kingdom, that has a ring of dark fur around each of its brown eyes. Weight: 9-11lb (4.1−5kg).

## British Giant

This is the largest British rabbit. A long, flat body is desired in this breed and the head is broad with ears held erect. The muscles should be firm all over the body, as excessive fat and bagginess are not required. Colours can be white with blue or pink eyes; black with brown or blue eyes; dark steel-grey with brown eyes; brown with blue-grey or brown eyes; or blue (fur) with blue, grey or brown eyes. Weight: does not less than 12½lb (5.68kg), bucks not less than 11½lb (5.23kg). Over 15lb (6.82kg) to gain 10 points on the show-bench. However, heavier weights than this have been recorded.

## Californian

A big rabbit bred mainly for meat. Rather splendid in appearance and docile enough to make a nice pet if you have a large hutch. The body is white with dark colour points on nose, ears, feet and tail. Weight: American Standard 8−10lb. (3.6−4.5kg), British Standard 8−10½lb (3.6−4.8kg).

## Chinchilla

This is a lovely rabbit with an intriguing coat. The fur is marked with bands of colour. If you blow gently into the fur, or part it carefully with the hands, each hair can be seen to have layers of colour: dark slate, followed by a band of pearl-white, followed by a top colour of black. This gives a grey ripple effect to the coat, which is very attractive. The fur is also soft and silky to touch. The body is short and cobby — altogether a pretty rabbit, which makes a good choice for a pet. Weight: 5½ − 7lb (2.5−3.1kg).

*Chinchilla Giganta:*
English weight — 8½ − 12lb (3.9−5.5kg).
German weight — 12lb (5.5kg).
American weight — 15lb (6.8kg).

## Dutch

One of the most popular fancy breeds which are kept purely as pets. The adults are usually docile when well-handled.

According to Ronald Lockley, author of *The Island,* the Dutch pattern of dark back, cheeks and ears, with a white saddle and blaze down the front of the head, occurs now and again in the wild.

Baby Dutch rabbits can be selected as having potential show quality at a young age, as the correct markings are present when the kittens are still in the nest. Some breeders do not rear the badly marked youngsters. The white blaze needs to be smoothly wedge-shaped with no irregular patches on a show specimen, but so often the white neck-band or saddle is broken by coloured hairs. The Dutch pattern is allowed in any of eight colours with white. The colours are black, blue, chocolate, brown-grey, pale-grey, steel-grey, tortoiseshell, or yellow. The black and the blue are the most popular and these two colours are often bred together to improve the intensity of shades. Whatever the colour, the coat of the Dutch lies smooth and shiny sleek. Weight: 4½ − 5lb (2.1−2.3kg).

## English

The English is another very popular pet and fancy rabbit. It is recognized in five colours: black, blue, tortoiseshell, chocolate, and grey. The coloured markings appear on nose, eyes, ears and a chain of spots along the sides on an otherwise white fur. The eyes are dark.

One of the most intriguing facts about the English breed is that the desired pattern occurs only in the heterozygous form (see Genetics, p.67)

The doe of this breed is often chosen as a foster-mother for the young of another doe. Some breeders arrange to have more than one doe kindle on the same day, so that if trouble shows up with, say, a valuable first-time doe, the kittens can be transferred to another nest and saved. It has been thought that some breeds have better maternal instincts than others, and that English does make good mothers. Weight: 6 − 8lb (2.7−3.6kg).

## Flemish Giant

An enormous rabbit that has a strong following of keen enthusiasts. The colour is dark steel-grey. When considering this breed, it is as well to remember that a very large hutch will be needed. Specimens over 21lb. (10kg) have been recorded.

## Harlequin

Here we have a handsome breed — medium to large in size and friendly in nature. The pattern of the coat is spectacular. One ear is black, the other is orange. The head is equally divided, one half orange and the other half black — the opposite way round to the ears. The legs are one black and one orange in front and the same but the opposite way round at the back. The body is banded in black and orange. There is also a brown-and-orange variety, or lilac and fawn, or blue and fawn. The black is the most popular, although the Harlequin is not a common breed in any colour. It is in fact quite rare and an interesting rabbit to breed. Recently, all the above colours with white instead of orange or fawn have been reintroduced and the variety is known as *Magpie,* i.e. black and white, blue and white, etc. There is also a Rexed type (with very short fur) in all the colours. Another feature of the Harlequins is their four or five inch long ears, which are carried so gracefully. Weight: 6−8lb (2.7−3.6kg).

## Havana

It is easy to see how fanciers fall for this breed with such lovely fur. The rich, dark-chocolate coat lies one inch in length all over and it is very dense on a compact body. In the Grand Exhibition at the Crystal Palace in 1910 this breed was given a guaranteed class. The breed is still popular with a specialist club and many first-class animals are to be seen at shows. The eyes are dark, but they have a distinct ruby glow. Weight: 6lb (2.7kg).

## Himalayan

This beautiful breed, which originated in Northern India and China, is recommended to those attracted to a patterned rabbit. The markings are similar to the points of a Siamese cat. The nose should be as dark as possible — the colour continuing well up between the eyes. The ears, tail and feet should be deeply coloured to match; but often the feet tend to be lighter than the ears and nose. The fur should be pure-white and the eyes pink like the true albino. It is a long breed with a slender body (sometimes described as 'snaky') and a fine head. Baby Himalayans are all-white at birth and they remain white while they are in the warm nest.

The dark points gradually appear during the six weeks after they leave the nest. It is difficult to pick out a promising youngster much before it is eight weeks old. Colours allowed by the Standard are black, blue, lilac, chocolate, on otherwise white fur. Weight: 4½−5lb. (2−2.3kg).

## Lilac

The dove-pink shade should be even all over the coat, right down to the skin, in the Lilac breed. It is a pretty rabbit, developed in England between 1913 and 1920. At one time it was known as the *Essex Lavender;* but also (in 1922) as the *Cambridge Blue,* due to the fact that the breed was produced by a geneticist at Cambridge. Nowadays Lilacs breed true, although it should be noted that a blue shade will be considered a fault on the show-table. Weight: 5½−7lb (2.5−3.2kg).

## Lop

A great favourite this large fellow. Long ears sweep down to the hutch floor either side of the rabbit's head. In the past there has been strong competition to see which breeder could produce the longest ears. However, the heavy head with elegant Roman nose can look rather pathetic if the ears are *too* long. There are now four main types: the *English Lop, French Lop, Dwarf Lop* and *German Meissner.*

*English Lop:* Has been known to weigh more than 20lb (9kg) and ear lengths of 30in (75cm) have been recorded. The ears do not start to drop until the babies are a few weeks old and youngsters then creep about with one ear up and the other ear down. This gives them a slightly puzzled expression.

*French Lop:* Has an easily recognized dip in the centre of the crown. The head with the correct shape of crown is important in a show specimen. The body is massive with thick-set muscles, but it is not as big as the English Lop. Weight: 10−12lb (4.6−5.4kg) upwards.

*Dwarf Lop:* Is becoming more popular. The ears, which measure 11−12½in (27.5−31cm), droop but they do not reach the ground and they seem more natural than the sweeping ears of the English Lop. Weight: 4.1lb (1.8kg).

*Meissner Lop:* Has a coat that is ticked all over with light-coloured hairs, otherwise the over-all body colour is black, blue, brown, yellow, etc. All the colours are recognized. Weight: 7−8lb (3.2−3.6kg).

**Netherland Dwarf**

This delightful little rabbit has an ear length of less than 2in (5cm). The tiny ear is definitely one of the distinguishing features of a good example of the breed. The other points to look for are very large bold eyes, a compact body, a round head with a nose short and flat to the face like a kitten, and soft roll-back fur. The adult buck can sit on the palm of an out-stretched hand. Poor quality Dwarfs are sometimes seen that exhibit none of these points and are quite ordinary. If, for example, the ears are long and the eyes are small, the rabbit does not have the same appeal.

The Netherland Dwarf has become more popular in recent years, perhaps for reasons of economy. Two adults can be kept *comfortably* in the space needed to house one medium-sized rabbit of another breed. Two to four adult Dwarfs will require only the amount of food needed by one rabbit of a medium-sized breed. There are other advantages: the Dwarf is easily handled and it is bred in many colours and patterns. This breed is certainly favoured by the owners of pet-shops, as the young rabbits leave the cages almost as fast as they come in! Apparently the coloured varieties are even more popular than the whites — there are two kinds of white: blue-eyed and pink-eyed. There are more than twenty-five colours available, ranging from the wild agouti shades to the exquisite Himalayan Dwarf (like a miniature Siamese cat) with dark nose, ears, tail and stockings. However, if you fancy a particular colour, you will probably have to go to a specialist breeder. The ideal weight is 2lb (0.9kg), but many are 2¼lb (1kg).

**New Zealand Black**

This variety was developed in the U.S.A. from a cross between the New Zealand Red and the New Zealand White. The first cross between a white buck and a red doe was made in the United States in 1947, but the breed was not officially recognized until 1958. It is a curious fact, however, that the British New Zealand Black was developed separately during the 1960s. It proved more difficult to obtain the desired result in Britain. In later years, the Alaska has been used to improve the blackness of the coat, but the perfect New Zealand Black is still to be bred. Weight: 9−12lb (4.1−5.5kg).

**New Zealand Red**

The exciting colour of this breed originates from a cross made between the Belgian Hare and the Golden Fawn in America early in the century. It is a bright golden red and quite different in type as well as colour from the better known White (below). The Red is longer and leaner with an arched back. The White has been bred from the Red. Weight: 8lb (3.6kg).

## New Zealand White
In spite of its large size and the fact that it was bred mainly for the meat and fur markets, a rabbit of this breed makes a good pet, as both bucks and does are usually fairly docile. The fur is dense and white, giving the rabbit a cuddly look that most children like. The broad head and thick, well-furred ears also add to the attractive appearance. Weight: 9−11lb (4.1−5kg).

## Polish
The Polish, although a small rabbit, differs considerably in type from the Netherland Dwarf. For one thing, it is not so cobby; it has a neat, sprightly appearance and a longer head — much more like a small version of a Belgian Hare. Another main difference is seen in the list of faults for the show rabbit: a roll-back coat is not favoured for Polish, whereas it is desired in the Dwarf. In the U.S.A. the Polish breed is known as the *Britannia Petit.* The red-eyed white variety is mostly seen, but there are as many colours available as for the Dwarfs. Weight: under 2½lb (1.1kg).

## Rex
A varied collection of rabbits come under this heading, as the word 'Rex' refers to the type of coat. Early in the 20th century, a rabbit appeared in France without the usual *long* guard hairs. This new kind of rabbit proved to be a mutation from the normal rabbit, that is the genes for the Rex coat were passed on as a hereditary factor. The new breed was called *Castor-rex.* Later, the Castor-rex was crossed with other rabbits to produce the short, velvety coat in many colours. Some of these colours are extremely popular today and special breed clubs for individual colours have been formed. The Rex breed has sub-divisions as follows:

*Self Rex:* To include rabbits of one all-over colour, e.g. Ermine (white), Black, Blue, Havana, Lilac, etc.

*Shaded:* To include rabbits with a dark saddle which is lighter in colour on the back towards the tail, and on the flanks, e.g. Smoke Pearl, Siamese Sable.

*Patterned:* To include tans and fox rabbits (see below for normal fur breeds in these colours).

*Marked:* To include Californian Rex, Dalmation Rex (spotted with dark ears), Harlequin Rex (see also above), Himalayan Rex, Magpie Rex. Weight: 6−8lb (2.7−3.6kg).

*Astrex:* At the present time, several rabbit fanciers are trying to reproduce this breed which had a coat that was tightly curled all over its body. It was originally produced in the 1930s and later exhibited in many of the normal rabbit colours. A similar breed, the *Oppossum Rex,* appeared in 1924. This rabbit had a loosely curled coat and it was rather striking. It is difficult to see why it was not more popular.

## Sable (normal length fur)
*Siamese Sable:* An English or French rabbit in spite of the name. There are light, medium, and dark shades. The fur is soft and very dense.

*Marten Sable:* A similar rabbit to the Siamese Sable in type, but with the sepia colour only on the back, ears and face. The eye circle, inside of ears, under jaw line, underneath, and undertail to be white. Again, there are light, medium, and dark forms; all shades are ticked with white hairs along the flanks. Weight: 5−7lb (2.3−3.2kg).

## Satin
A rabbit of this breed has a special kind of hair which occurred in the U.S.A. as a mutation from the normal coat. As the name 'Satin' implies, the fur is unusually shiny. The fur has a special texture and glossy sheen; and it is the actual structure of the hair cells that is different. The coat rolls softly back when stroked from tail to head. Satin rabbits in most colours are now available. Weight: 6−8lb (2.7−3.6kg).

## Siberian
A rabbit produced by crossing English and Dutch breeds. Colours can be black, brown, blue or chocolate — each variety to be free from white hairs. The fur is one inch (2.5cm) all over and of the roll-back kind. Weight: 5−7lb (2.3−3.2kg).

## Silver
Sometimes known as the *English Silver,* this breed is easily recognized by its rather thin, elegant shape and by the distinctive ticking of silver hairs all over otherwise dark fur. This silvering does not develop in the babies

until they are four to six weeks old. The first coats of the kittens are completely black, brown or fawn. The silver hairs begin to show more clearly after the first moult. Weight: 6lb (2.7kg).

## Silver Fox
This rabbit should not be confused by the novice with the *English Silver* above. Indeed, the Silver Fox is often simply referred to as the *Fox*. The fur is patterned like the Black and tan, only the tan colour has been replaced by white (see Tan). The silver ticking is limited in this rabbit to the sides of the body and flanks, and the edge of the jowls. It is a heavier type than the Tan. Weight: 5½ − 7lb (2.5−3.2kg).

## Smoke Pearl (Normal)
A medium-sized breed with dark face-mask and ears. The saddle, face, ears, feet and upper side of tail are smoke-grey; but this deep colour shades to an even pearl-grey on the sides, flanks and chest. A popular choice for exhibition and a rabbit of this breed makes a good-looking pet. Weight: 5−7lb (2.3−3.2kg).

## Tan
The Black-and-tan rabbit occurred as a mutant in Derby in 1887. There has been some friendly disagreement among fanciers recently over the Standard regarding the pattern of the black and tan areas of fur. Basically, the head and cheeks are black with a tan circle round each eye, and the back and upper side of tail are black. The chest, nose, belly and undertail are golden tan. The area of dispute is the triangle of tan colour behind the ears. This should be present but the exact width of the area has been queried. The Blue–and–tan was first introduced in England during 1922, quickly followed by the Chocolate-and-tan. Ten years later, the Lilac-and-tan was produced from a crossing between a Chocolate-and-tan and a Blue-and-tan. Weight: approximately 4½ lb (2kg). This breed makes a brave and cheerful little pet.

## Tri-Dutch
An interesting breed for those who like something multicoloured. It is a combination of the Dutch pattern and the Harlequin markings. More like the Dutch in type and size, it carries the typical white blaze down the front of the face, while one cheek is orange and the other black, with opposite colours on the ears, as in the Harlequin. The front half of the body, or saddle, is pure-white; the back half of the body is banded in orange and black. It is very difficult to breed a rabbit with the correct

*Young rabbits—three weeks old*

*Prize-winning Smoke Pearl Netherland Dwarf*

*Best English at Bradford 1979 owned by F. Proctor*

*English Lop owned by Clipsham Bros.*

*Red-eyed White Polish—Best of Breed at Bradford 1979 owned by S. Cole*

*Blue Dutch owned by J. Barker*

*Belgian Hare buck—Best of Breed at Bradford 1979 owned by George Hardstaff*

markings, and anything less than perfect is patterned more like a tortoise-shell-and-white cat. Weight:   approximately 4−5½ lb (1.8−2.5kg).

# Housing

Basically, there are four ways in which you can house your pet rabbits. However, there are many variations on each of the basic designs.

Let us call type one the wire cage, type two the simple wooden hutch for use under cover, type three the outdoor hutch, and type four the triangular-shaped hutch for placing on the grass.

Right from the beginning, it is best to consider whether you are going to keep your rabbits inside or outside, as the decision might influence your choice of hutch or cage. Some types will be satisfactory for rabbits that are kept in a waterproof shed or garage; other types should only be chosen for a rabbitry where the temperature is controlled; and yet others are suitable for outdoor use.

It is also a good idea to consider carefully what kind of housing you are going to need *before* you buy your stock. If you decide to build a hutch yourself, it could take as long as a week and you will want to have it ready for when the new rabbit or rabbits arrive.

The all-wire cage is used commercially for the breeding of meat rabbits. It is designed for arranging in stacks and or rows inside a rabbitry built especially to allow for controlled temperature and humidity. Therefore, it need not concern the person who keeps rabbits simply as pets.

Another way of keeping rabbits inside is to make use of a garden shed with wide windows that let in lots of light. It is preferable if these can be opened to allow fresh air to circulate freely during spring, summer, autumn or fall, and most of the winter months. In other words, rabbits like *and need* plenty of fresh air. There will be few days when you have to keep the windows  tightly  closed  all  day − only when it is icy cold.

Another site that often proves suitable is under a barn-like roof that is open on all sides but sheltered from above. A garage can be adapted to make a satisfactory rabbitry, providing it is not to be used for a car. Your pets could be killed by the petrol fumes if car and rabbits are housed together.

A stable makes a comfortable home for pet rabbits, but again they are very sensitive to fumes from the manure, and dust from the quantities of hay and straw that are forked around if horses are in residence; and it has been found difficult to keep rabbits healthy in lofts above stables, but a disused stable can be adapted to give shelter to rabbit hutches.

It is not sensible to keep a rabbit in a greenhouse or conservatory through spring and summer even if you put up shade. A hutch behind glass becomes extremely hot, even in the early spring, and rabbits have heavy coats. However, sometimes a hutch can be carried into a corner of a conservatory in late autumn or fall for the worst of the winter, and carried outside again in very early spring before the first rays of strong sunshine come through the glass.

If a rabbit is seen lying on one side breathing quickly and the atmosphere seems warm, then you have left the move too late. Even in winter, the windows must be left open, otherwise the air becomes heavy and damp — fatal to many forms of life. It is worth repeating that rabbits must have fresh air to survive. Some breeders would claim that it is never recommended to house rabbits in a glasshouse or conservatory but, in my experience, providing they are only kept under glass during the cold months and so long as they are given plenty of fresh air, rabbits can be more comfortable out of driving rain and freezing winds.

Remember also that when you spray your plants during winter, if a pest-killer or disease-preventative of any kind is used, the rabbit must be taken out of the conservatory first, as the chemicals might be harmful.

Other places around the home where you can site a hutch include: a position against a south-facing fence or wall in the garden; on a balcony; in a backyard or outhouse; or simply to one side of a path. It is not advisable to keep a hutch in the family house, although it is possible to house-train a pet rabbit for short visits indoors. Rabbits are naturally quite clean animals in their habits if they are given a chance, i.e., if they are used to clean conditions every day in their own hutch with regular removal of the soiled shavings, sawdust, newspaper, etc. that build up in one corner. The rabbit's brain is rather small and your pet will be slow to understand your wishes. All that can be said is that with patience you can train a rabbit to use one newspaper, box of sawdust, or area of a dwelling rather than the whole floor. To smack a rabbit for making any kind of mistake is senseless. The bones are extremely fragile and easily broken.

### Cage or hutch?

The hutch for use inside a shed need only be simple because it should be amply protected from wind and rain by the outer building. A single hutch for one pet buck or doe could be made to stand on its own legs, or two or three hutches could be arranged in the form of a stack. The latter might be a solitary unit fixed beside other similar units of two or three compartments, or it might be two single hutches stacked one on top of the other.

The single wooden hutch is usually an oblong box shape with a wire netting front on a frame. The front may lift right out or swing open on a hinge like a door or window. In either case, it is best if there is a litter board to prevent the bedding from falling out.

The doe with young will need a larger hutch than a maiden doe or a buck. The breeding hutch can be built like a small flat for the doe with an open living room and boarded-in bedroom. However, some breeders like to use a double-size hutch without a closed-in compartment, although in this case a nesting box is placed on one side.

If the hutch is to go on a balcony, some adaptations are necessary for the occupant during inclement weather. Always remember wet conditions are worse for a rabbit than cold, but some form of shield from freezing cold winds is essential. Choose a corner out of the wind and, if possible, face the hutch towards the south. Have one side boarded over, and preferably choose or make a model with an enclosed sleeping compartment. Fix a sheet of heavy-duty polythene to the underside of the roof, so that it is ready to hang down over the open section when it rains. The whole structure should have 9in (22.5cm) legs attached so that the floor is raised above the damp of the ground.

Hutches required for a place in the garden where there will not be a roof overhead should be of sound construction. They will need all the protective items mentioned above and, in addition, the roof of the hutch should slant to allow rain-water to drain away from the front. It helps if it is made larger at the front and back than the top of the hutch, as this stops a flood of water running into the inside when it rains really hard. Again, legs to raise the outdoor hutch are important and a polythene cover for the front is extremely useful. It is a good idea to build shutters for the wire netting part of the door for winter.

Another way of giving your pet extra comfort in winter is to cut out a square from a large cardboard box to push into the wire frame every night during the coldest months. If a polythene sheet is hung down over this, the same sheet of card will last all winter. A rain-soaked piece of card will deteriorate quickly, and as this will fall out during the night, it is useless anyway. The polythene will keep the card dry and stiff, but remember to leave the rabbit an air-hole.

If a hard frost is expected and snow is driving down when it is time to feed and close up the rabbits for the night, enough air should get through if one corner of the card is turned back, i.e. a card is pushed into the entire frame at the front of the hutch with only one corner bent down; a polythene sheet is hung over the outside of the card and weighted at the bottom. If wooden shutters are used, card is not necessary.

Incidentally, while mentioning frost and sleet, it is as well to make an outdoor hutch with the coldest winter day in mind — the worst weather can be quite difficult to imagine when knocking up a hutch on a sunny afternoon in summer! Your poor rabbit will surely suffer if the wood is not thick enough to keep out the cold, and the roof not wide enough to keep out the rain.

There is yet another type of basic hutch and this is the one that has a wire run built onto the side. This type is often called the Morant hutch, especially if constructed in a triangular shape with a wooden floor under a boarded-in section. The run section has a wire netting floor in addition to the wire netting sides. This is to prevent the rabbit digging holes in the grass. Rabbits less than a year old are very good at escaping! They spend their time looking for the smallest gap in the wire or framework and they will jump and squeeze through what seem to be the most unlikely places. Older rabbits settle down to a quiet munch on the grass. It seems that they cannot be bothered to try and escape. Also older rabbits become most conservative. They do not like change. In a happy home they remain quiet and contented.

All rabbits like exercise. They enjoy going out in a run, so even if you do not favour the Morant type of hutch, if you own any kind of lawn or grass patch, you might consider making a wire run without a sleeping section. This simple structure is merely a wooden frame with wire netting on every side, including the base. The top can have a frame lid that lifts right off or hinges back for convenience.

On warm sunny days all the year round, the pet rabbit is taken out of his regular hutch, where it sleeps every night, and carried gently to its garden run. Sometimes as early as before breakfast it can be popped inside, and may need no more attention until bedtime, other than a folded deckchair placed on top to protect him from the sun. Some form of shade will become necessary on nearly all summer days. Rabbits feel hot in their heavy fur coats and should *never* be left in scorching sun without shade.

In winter, pet rabbits should not be put out in grass runs when the ground is absolutely soaking, when there is an icy wind blowing, or when the ground is frosty.

## Sizes
If you hope to keep healthy, happy rabbits, make sure your hutches are

large enough. One of the worst faults that occur where new owners are concerned involves the size of hutch. It is amazing how so many beginners think that a rabbit will be comfortable for weeks and weeks, or perhaps its entire life-time, in a cage where it can hardly turn round. There is no doubt that a rabbit with a roomy hutch, large enough to allow a little hopping up and down, will be a much happier animal and a more docile pet.

A domestic rabbit does not appear to mind living in its own little hutch — providing the box is of a reasonable size. It is difficult to give exact measurements for one pet, as breeds vary considerably in weight and length. Tame rabbits can be tiny 2¾lb (1.2kg) Dwarfs, or massive giants. Hutches to suit most medium-sized breeds should be *not less than* 3ft x 2ft x 18in (90cm x 60cm x 45cm), or for Dwarfs 2ft x 2ft x 18in (60cm x 60cm x 45cm). This is for *one* pet.

Breeding hutches are made longer and wider than general stock hutches, i.e. a larger hutch will be needed for a breeding doe than for a single maiden doe, a resting doe, or a buck. The extra space is essential as the mother doe must have room to manage her litter and move about the floor without treading on her kittens. The breeding hutch will be housing a full-size doe plus six or seven youngsters for several weeks. Therefore, it is a good idea to consider these details when purchasing or making your first hutch; otherwise, as so often happens, another hutch will have to be obtained at a later date, when the children beg you to let their bunny have some babies.

Sometimes the available space is divided into two in order to provide a sleeping compartment (where the doe will probably deposit her young) and a living area. The sleeping area usually has a solid wooden door or boarded-in front, while the living end has a completely removable wire frame or hinged door.

However, some breeders like to use a loose nest-box in an open cage, rather than a separate compartment. It is really a matter of personal choice, although nearly every doe likes to have some form of privacy during kindling and the early stages of rearing a litter. Rabbits are shy animals.

**How to make a hutch**

You will need a supply of wood. This can be purchased from a wood merchant, or perhaps you will be able to adapt an old wooden cupboard. If you decide to buy new materials, ask for tongued and grooved boards and get the lengths of wood cut to the sizes that you require. This helps to make the job easier for the non-carpenter.

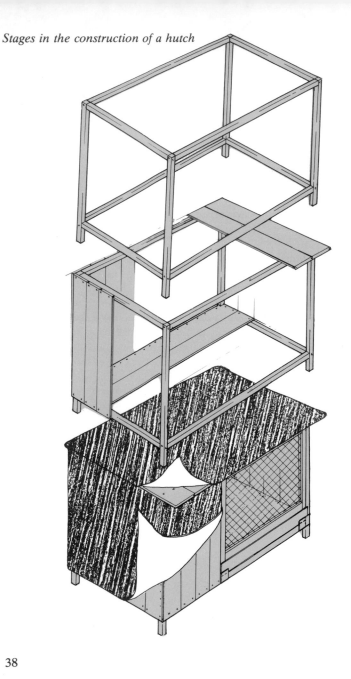

*Stages in the construction of a hutch*

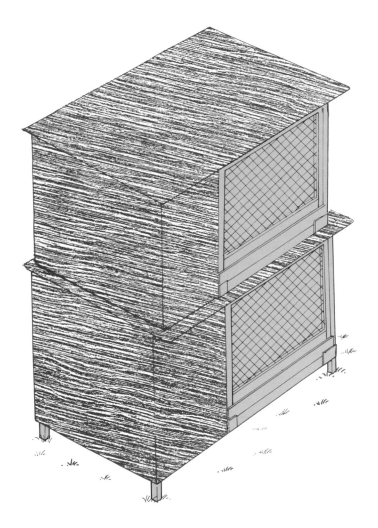

*Hutches may be stacked, or made in one unit*

The first step in making a hutch concerns the size. In many cases, this will depend upon the breed of rabbit which is to be kept as a pet (see above). A hutch is basically a box with two sides, a back, a roof, a base, and a wire mesh on a frame front door. The roof of an outdoor hutch should slope from front to back by at least 1in (2.5cm) and it should also hang over the front to prevent rain-water running down into the hutch. Legs, or some other form of support, will be needed to raise the hutch floor 6—9in (15—22.5cm) above ground — essential if the rabbit is to be protected from frost and damp.

Having decided on the size of the hutch, it is always advisable to draw a three-dimensional sketch; this helps when you come to work out the right quantity of wood required.

When you have purchased the wood, galvanised nails, wire mesh and waterproof felt, the next step is to construct the frame. Then nail the boards to the sides and the back, followed by the floor, part of the front of the hutch (not wider than 1ft (30cm)), and finally the roof.

At this stage, you can construct either a door with hinges, or a drop-in door onto a removable litter board to ease the cleaning of the hutch, as shown in figure 3. The door could either be secured by a latch, bolt, or a button, depending on the preference of the individual. However, do see that this is firm enough to prevent cats and/or foxes from opening the cage. Many such cases are reported every year.

On completion make the hutch weather-proof by covering the roof, back, both sides, and the front section, with roofing felt.

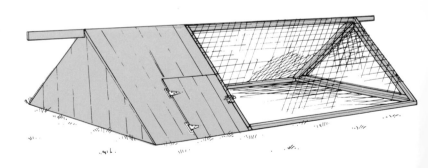

*Morant hutch*

# Equipment

The new rabbit-keeper's major purchase in the way of equipment will obviously be the hutch. Besides this, there are some other items that are necessary and others that will be found useful. Necessary items include feeding pots; water bowls or bottles; a hutch-scraper and bucket for cleaning out; bins for storing food. Optional extras include:   shelves, hay racks, nest-boxes, travelling-boxes, wire floor trays, tables for grooming, vacuum-blowers for angoras. Breeders or owners of pet angoras might also like to consider spinning-wheels and weaving-looms, but these luxury items are for the specialists that aim to make their own wool up into home-made garments (see section on Angoras).

**Feeding pots**
It is best if these are fairly heavy and not to be flicked over by a rabbit. A plastic margarine or cottage cheese carton is a useful size, but most rabbits will turn these over with their teeth or bite holes in the base. There should be space for every youngster to feed in comfort. Where there is a large litter, a long trough might be found better than a round pot. The shape and material of the container should be simple, to permit easy cleaning. China, earthenware or heavy plastic are all used. Metal troughs and clip-on cups may also be purchased. If you decide to have a container that hangs on the wire front of the cage, bunny will probably delight in unhooking it every day! In my own experience heavy earthenware pots have proved to be the most useful, with plastic cartons for emergencies only. The one advantage here is that they are not expensive and can be thrown away after a day or two. This can be a hygenic timesaver when dealing with a sick rabbit.

**Water bowls and bottles**
There is a fairly new bowl design that consists of two bowls in a continuous plastic unit — one to be used for water and the other for pellets. These are sometimes favoured by pet shops, presumably because they are convenient. My main criticism is that they tend to be large, which means

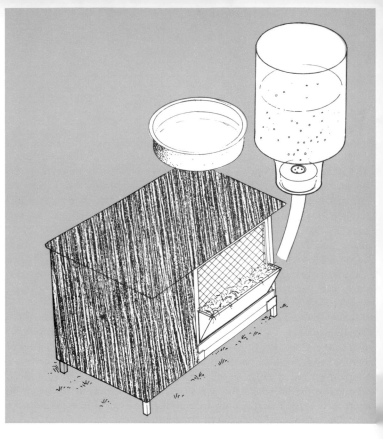

*Hay rack, drinking bottle, and bowl for water*

that they take up much of the hutch floor area. This is all right if the hutch is really large, but it is rather a sorry sight to see animals that can only make one hop from bed to dirty corner — and this over an out-size feed and water unit! On the other hand, the containers must be large enough. One way of getting round the problem is to use a glass or plastic bottle that hangs on the *outside* of the hutch with the nipple pointing through the wire front. Both have advantages and disadvantages — namely, glass bottles drop and break from time to time even in the hands of the most careful pet-owner. Plastic bottles do not break so easily (although even these *do* crack or split sometimes if dropped), but they tend to expand and contract on warm days, which causes water to drip into the hutch. Both kinds are inclined to go green inside from minute plant growths, unless carefully brushed at regular intervals.

Many breeders still prefer the more old-fashioned pot or bowl, and as long as these are washed out and refilled regularly, they are quite satisfactory. Whichever kind of drinking vessel is chosen, it should not be easy for the rabbit to spill the water, as a wet hutch is not only unpleasant to look at, but uncomfortable and unhealthy for the pet. Do not choose a deep pot for very young rabbits in case, in their efforts to drink, they fall in and drown.

### Hutch-scraper

We have a strong garden trowel with a wooden handle that does the job of clearing dirty corners very well, but there is a scraper on the market that has a triangular top and three straight sides and is excellent for getting into awkward hutch corners. A flat hand shovel with a short handle can be another useful tool for lifting wet saw-dust.

### Bucket

A large plastic bucket will be necessary if your pet's house is going to be kept reasonably fresh and sweet-smelling. Although comparatively few rabbit-breeders wash out their hutches with disinfectant after every cleaning session, it does help to prevent flies breeding if a thorough scrub is given regularly in summer. If the rabbit can be run out in a grass pen for two or three hours on a sunny day, this is a good time to do the job. The hutch should be quite dry before clean bedding is inserted. In any case, hutches should be disinfected before a new rabbit is introduced, or after any illness or death. When a litter has been weaned and removed, a few drops of disinfectant in the cleaning water makes all the difference to health and hygiene.

### Bins for storing food

Bins are necessary if your pets are not going to be contaminated by vermin. Rats and mice might be attracted to loose corn or paper packets of rabbit food mixtures. The most economical way to buy rabbit pellets and mixed corn is by the sack. It works out as the better buy even if you only have one pet. You will get is several pence or cents less per pound or kilogram. The best way to store food is in a new dustbin. If you can share a sack with a neighbour, or can obtain smaller quantities cheaply at your local pet shop, you can store oats and pellets in a biscuit or cake tin. We store ours in a large bin, transferring small amounts to a cake tin for daily use.

### Shelves

A section of wood fixed inside a large hutch halfway up one wall allows a buck some exercise jumping up and down, or a doe a chance to escape for a while from the demands of a growing litter. A shelf is best fitted into place when the hutch is being made.

### Hay racks

These can easily be made at home from narrow wire mesh folded into a V-shape and fixed to the side of the hutch. However, do be careful not to leave any sharp ends. Another kind of rack can be fixed to the *outside* of the wire door. Sometimes these mangers are seen in the form of wooden slats; but even one piece of wood arranged at an angle to the door can be filled with hay. The rabbit then pulls any amount of hay through the wire of the door. One danger here is that the bulk of hay might obstruct the light. Growing animals do best if they obtain plenty of daylight, so if in doubt, make sure that you feed hay in a clean part of the hutch.

### Nest-boxes

Separate loose boxes for kindling are liked by some does and rejected by others. Hutches that do not have a special boarded-off compartment should have a card fixed into one half of the door to give the doe some privacy during kindling. On this same side of the hutch, a nest-box can be slipped into place well before the date the doe's family is due. You cannot expect a doe to take to a strange box that is suddenly introduced into her hutch when she is shortly to give birth. Remember to allow plenty of time for the mother to get used to it. Some breeders provide no extra box at kindling time. The doe simply produces her kits in a corner, covering them with hay and fur. Few losses should occur, providing the rabbits are housed inside. Where outside hutches are used, the extra warmth obtained from the added thickness of a nest-box is undoubtedly beneficial and might save your baby rabbits from dying from cold.

The measurements of the box will obviously vary according to the size of the doe. Whatever the size. the sides should not be so deep that the doe could damage her milk glands getting in and out. The babies should also be able to hop in and out when just over two weeks old. 15in x 18in x 8in (37.5cm x 45cm x 20cm) is a standard size. However, Dwarfs do well with a shallow tray with a thick wooden base which makes a warm floor for the babies, but allows them to toddle in and out from an early age. One word of warning:   youngsters just beginning to creep out of the nest have been known to slip down between the hutch wall and the nest-box. Make sure this cannot happen, by stuffing any gaps with hay.

**Travelling-boxes**

These become necessary only if you wish to show your rabbit. The box should be light yet strong. The reason for the lightness is that rail charges depend on weight. The strength is for the rabbit's comfort. Besides travelling to shows by rail, rabbits are taken to shows all over the country by their owners. Sometimes the shows are situated fairly close to the rabbit owner's home and the box is carried by hand or placed on the back seat of a car. Boxes are constructed to hold one large rabbit or two, or three small ones — each in a partitioned-off section. (Incidentally, there is little fear that a rabbit will be allowed to suffer during transportation since a show specimen is a valuable animal in near perfect condition and much treasured by its owner.)

A simple shape of box is preferred with generous ventilation, either in the form of holes at each end or a ridge along the sides of the top. There are several satisfactory designs on the market (see Useful Addresses) but it is possible to make a box at home. The size chosen for a Dwarf or a Dutch should be about 14in x 8in x 12in (35cm x 20cm x 30cm). For a larger breed, such as an Angora, a French Lop or a New Zealand White, a box 18in x 12in x 14in (45cm x 30cm x 35cm) will be needed.

**Wire floor trays**

Frames fitted with firm wire mesh (not netting) are used as a false floor by some breeders. The idea is that the rabbit walks above its droppings and does not dirty its fur. The droppings fall through the wire onto a hard floor beneath. Angora breeders and commercial rabbit-keepers often recommend wire floors, but there are advantages and disadvantages. Wire floors can cause sore hocks, and chills through the base of the hutch. On the other hand, it helps to prevent disease if rabbits are unable to sit on their droppings, and it is slightly easier to clean cages with wire trays fitted above the floors. However, it should be noted that rabbits kept outside should have solid floors, as these are considerably warmer. Metal gets extremely cold during the winter.

**Tables for grooming**

A table becomes a necessity if you are thinking of showing even one super pet, but in any case, it is useful to have somewhere to place your rabbit when you take him from his hutch to make a routine health check. Spread a piece of sack to prevent the animal from sliding. A rabbit quickly loses confidence if its feet slip on a shiny surface. Show rabbits are removed from their hutches daily so that they become used to being handled and there is no doubt that if you pick your pet up frequently (and always very gently) it remains quiet and easy to manage. A rabbit that is handled daily by its owner usually learns to sit well for the judge. Angora rabbits must be groomed regularly and some owners prefer to do this with their pet on a table.

**Vacuum-blowers**
These are used to bring the coat of an Angora rabbit into perfect show condition. Every part of the wool should be free from tangles and there must be no matting. Regular daily attention is needed to achieve successful results.

# Feeding

An animal that is correctly fed will always make a better pet. A rabbit that is well-nourished and content is more likely to be docile. The coat and eyes will be bright and shining with health. An attractive pet is the result of a regular, daily feeding programme.

There are two major points to keep in mind. Firstly, rabbits do not thrive if there are too many sudden changes. If you can give them their food at approximately the same time, or times, every day, this will be a definite step in the right direction towards success. You could, for example, always feed before work and after tea. It is surprising how quickly pets respond to regular timing and wait at the front of their cages watching, waiting, and above all, listening. They can recognise the slightest rattle of the bag, tin, or sack in which their food is kept — even if it is a considerable distance away from the hutches in kitchen, shed, garage or stable. If by chance their owner happens to be standing close by the hutches and someone else opens the feed container at the other end of the garden, yard, etc., the owner sees the rabbit's ears move in response to the distant sounds.

Secondly, remember that rabbits need a constant supply of roughage in their diet. This means that even if you are providing plenty of food at meal times, there should always be a supply of fresh hay or good quality straw for them to munch in between times. Rabbits have a special kind of intestine (gut) that can break down cellulose, but their digestive system works best if there is a steady passage of food passing through the alimentary canal. Rabbits are quite fussy about the cleanliness of their hay or straw. They do not normally pick it up from the floor of the hutch and eat it after it has been heavily walked on or soiled, that is unless they are desperate from being near to starvation. Therefore, it is not a good idea to fill the hutch up with hay or straw once a week and expect the poor creature to eat his way through the pile for seven days. Hay should be placed in the hutch once a day as part of the diet. It is better if the daily supply can be put into a hay rack off the floor in a large hutch, but not if it is going to take precious exercise space in a small one. Also, beware of wire loops for hay, as it has been known for a rabbit to hang itself in this kind of contraption.

Another point about hay to watch, especially in winter, is that if hay is used for bedding as well as food, sometimes a pet will eat its whole supply by nightfall and be left with nothing for a mattress. It can happen with straw too, so it is necessary to be generous with bedding in cold weather, although rabbits do not eat straw quite so quickly as hay, as it is slightly less palatable to them.

Rabbits are herbivorous animals. They will eat many kinds of green-foods, cereals and roots. In addition to raw vegetables and uncooked cereals, they appreciate bits of human food, such as a slice of toast or brown bread, the scrapings from the porridge saucepan (when cool of course), rice pudding leftovers, etc., and some pets have been known to develop a taste for digestive biscuits!

Nowadays, breeders often feed their stock with commercial rabbit pellets which are carefully prepared from a balanced mixture of carbo-hydrates, proteins, fats, minerals and vitamins. Quite a number of rabbits prefer one brand of pellets to another and it is soon noticed that a change in brands causes feeding pots to be left half full. Any change in a rabbit's diet should be gradual.

A rabbit of a medium-sized breed will need about a cupful of pellets a day, unless in kindle when twice this amount will be required. A doe with six week old youngsters should be given three times her usual ration.

Pet-owners often ask if they can feed their rabbits on household left-overs. This is possible where only one or two pets are involved, but it must be remembered that if bread and scraps of pudding etc. are to form the major part of the diet, they will need to be given in more generous quantities than just tit-bits. For example, a large slice of bread or a good handful of crusts, plus greenfood, will be necessary every day, not just when they happen to be stale or otherwise available.

Some rabbits will take bread and milk, but it seems to be a matter of individual taste, as others will not touch it. When liked, this is a treat greatly appreciated by does with young, especially in the colder months, and it helps the doe to provide enough milk of her own for the babies. Normally, rabbits tend to choose dry, crisp foods in place of wet, sloppy dishes, if they get the chance.

When thinking about your new rabbit's diet, it is as well to know the basic food requirements:

*Carbohydrates* are needed to provide energy. They are found in breads

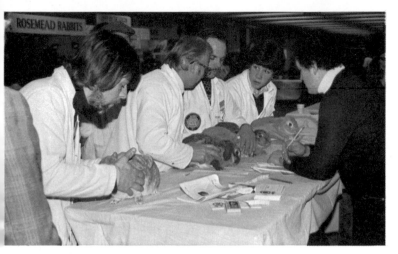

*Dwarf French Lops on the judging table*

*Rabbit using a drinking bottle*

*Doe with young in makeshift run on grass. Polythene is NOT recommended as a substitute for wire netting*

*Blanc de Bouscat owned by Mr. Toon-Poynton*

*School pet Dutch buck on holiday*

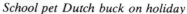

and cereals. If too much of these foods is taken, the surplus will turn into fat in the animal's body.

*Proteins* are used to build up the lean body tissue (and the young if the doe is in kindle). Wild rabbits get their protein from fresh green grass and young leaves. A rabbit with young enjoys an extra handful of grass every day. It helps her to provide enough milk (which is high in protein content) for her babies. Rabbit pellets also contain protein and more of these and less corn should be given to feeding does or does in kindle.

All rabbits need *roughage* and this is given as hay or straw as already explained. The necessary *minerals* will be in a mixed diet of greenfood, roots and hay, even if the rabbit is not fed pellets. *Vitamins* are important in the diet. *Vitamin A,* found in grass, cabbage, sprouts, carrots, and many other garden plants and weeds, protects against infection. *Vitamin B,* present in cereals, protects against nervous illnesses. *Vitamin C,* found in greenfoods such as grass, cabbage, lettuce, etc., is not normally a problem with rabbits. *Vitamin D* is the sunshine vitamin and there is usually no trouble with rickets or weak bones if young rabbits have some sunlight during the day (although shade is always necessary on a warm or hot day). *Vitamin E* is associated with fertility in humans as well as rabbits and freshly sprouted cereals and other seeds are particularly rich in this vitamin. A rabbit with a regular amount of green grass or leaves in its diet will not need specially sprouted seeds.

Although rabbits do not like sudden complete changes, they do appreciate variety in their diet. Many breeders feed nothing but pellets and perhaps in some cases hay (with water of course), but a mixed diet will be just as satisfactory and probably preferred by your pet. Certainly, if the rabbit is used to variety and a mixed diet, it will not react to change in the way that it would if fed mainly on two or three items, such as pellets and hay, or pellets, corn and hay, for a long period.

Some pet-owners like to feed a mixture of bread, cereals, pellets, etc. in the morning and different greenfoods at night with hay *ad lib.* at all times. Others choose to feed cereals etc. in the early morning, greens at lunchtime, with a handful of hay at night. A third way is to feed a generous quantity of greens in the morning, with a cereal/pellets feed plus hay at night. However, many breeders give just one feed of pellets per day with hay at the same time.

The best way to judge how much food should be given is to watch the individual pet's appetite. A well-fed rabbit should look eager for its food when you go to the hutch at meal times, yet there should be one or two pellets present in the dish right up until almost the time for the following meal. After a few days of careful observation, a sympathetic pet-owner soon learns exactly how much is being eaten. There should be no waste. If the dish is half full when it is time to feed again, cut down considerably the amount given. Over-feeding is not economical. A hutch half full of stale food is horrible to look at and not good for the rabbit's health. Remove anything that is not eaten overnight, or if pellets are left, miss the next meal.

Rabbits eat more at night than in the day, so if only one feed can be managed, try to make it an evening feed. Does carrying or suckling young should always be given two feeds a day.

It is possible to keep a rabbit entirely on greenfood, but it is not always realized what an enormous quantity of green grass, weeds, vegetables and tree clippings a rabbit can get through in a day, if this is the only type of food. Also, if you decide to give your pet a diet of greens make the change gradually. For example, add more and more grass and leaf trimmings every day for a week, while cutting down on the cereals a fraction each day. In such a case, try to include a large variety of different kinds of plants from the following list: vegetable peelings, sprout tops, carrot tops and tails, turnip tops, radish tops, dandelions, grass, trimmings from suitable trees and shrubs (see list below), kale or cabbage leaves, weeds (see list below). Remember, a tiny handful will not be nearly enough and that an all-green diet still needs to be supplemented with hay or straw at all times. Frozen plants should never be offered to rabbits, as digestive upsets are likely to occur if greens are not thawed out before feeding.

### Wild foods suitable for rabbits

*Blackberry brambles:* The young shoots and leaves are enjoyed by rabbits. They do not seem to mind the prickly thorns. The foliage has a health-giving effect. Also good for counteracting scours.

*Bindweed* (Convolvulus): Best fed mixed with other greens. A weed that is gladly fed to rabbits.

*Chickweed:* It is worth learning to recognize the common weed, as it is widespread and much enjoyed by pets.

*Clover:* In summer adult stock can take quite large amounts of clover with no ill effect, but it is a plant to watch out for when placing young stock into a grass run for the first time (or adults if they have not been accustomed to going outside). Large quantities of clover can cause bloat if introduced suddenly into a non-green diet. The gas produced during the digestive process can get trapped in the intestine and build up until pressure on the heart causes death.

*Comfrey:*  The benefits of this plant for humans as well as rabbits are becoming better known. It can be found growing wild in some areas, or cultivated in the garden.

*Dandelion:*  This is a favourite and it acts as a tonic. Do not feed too much at any one time and if possible mix the leaves with other green plants. An excellent plant to grow for the vitamins and minerals it contains.

*Grasses:*  All kinds are enjoyed by rabbits — even the creeping weed grass is well liked.

*Groundsel:*  Another suitable weed which can be found in most areas growing in abundance.

*Nettles:*  Very good when dried and fed as hay. The leaves contain useful proteins.

*Plantain:*  A rabbit favourite. Be careful not to gather plants from places where dogs might have fouled the area.

*Shepherd's purse:*  Many a breeder has gathered and dried this little weed and kept it for tempting a pet that appears one morning to be a little less lively than usual.

*Sow thistle:*  A juicy plant with succulent leaves and white milky sap in the stem. It is not so prickly as other thistles and the whole plant can be fed.

*Yarrow:*  A plant that is safe to feed to all stock — bucks, does, youngsters.

In addition to the plants listed above, thin branches and prunings of some shrubs and trees and most fruit bushes are enjoyed. Perhaps you grow a selection of the following: apple, birch, blackberry, hazel,

Kerria japonica (with yellow pompon flowers in spring), pear, raspberry, rose, willow (much liked). DO NOT FEED EVERGREEN SHRUBS AND TREES.

### Easy plants to grow at home for rabbits

Even if you are a keen gardener (and, contrary to what might be expected, many gardeners are rabbit-fanciers), the prospect of growing greens especially for rabbits might seem rather extraordinary. However, growing vegetables for yourself and family and giving the rabbits the trimmings is quite in order. For not only will you have health-giving vitamin-rich food, but your pets will benefit from the generous quantities of greens in their diet. If this notion should lead to a life-long interest in gardening, so much the better.

Vegetables to grow especially for rabbits include: chicory (grows tall and has beautiful blue flowers), comfrey (the leaves are full of protein), dandelions (young leaves are excellent for your salads too), kale (good for winter greens and comes in many colours).

It is possible to pick greens from the garden during every month of the year if careful attention is given to seed-sowing and harvesting times. Here are a few of the popular kinds of vegetables:

*Artichokes (Jerusalem):* These grow tall and leafy like hardy sunflowers. They are worth considering if space can be found where they can grow undisturbed — perhaps against an open-weave fence, where they will also provide some screening. The tubers are similar in appearance to knobbly potatoes. They may be boiled or roasted for humans to eat, or fed fresh to rabbits. The tubers can be left in the ground until they are required. Frost won't damage them. Any that remain undisturbed all winter will sprout again the following spring and provide a further supply of young tubers the next season, i.e. late autumn or early winter. Rabbits also enjoy the green leaves of this plant.

*Beans:* Runners are not fed when tough and stringy.

*Broccoli:* This is a fine vegetable for the family and a great standby for the cold months. Rabbits can be fed any trimmings.

*Cabbage:* All varieties are enjoyed by rabbits: plain green, curly, crinkly, purple, scarlet, and cream. Medium and large-sized breeds will even eat the thick stems and Dwarfs will do their best if the stems are split before feeding.

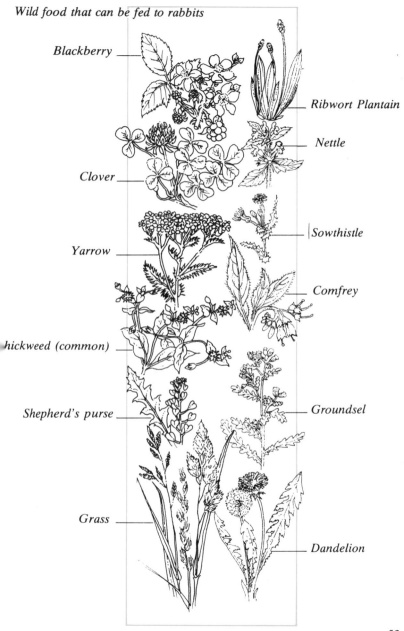

*Wild food that can be fed to rabbits*

Blackberry

Ribwort Plantain

Nettle

Clover

Yarrow

Sowthistle

Comfrey

Chickweed (common)

Shepherd's purse

Groundsel

Grass

Dandelion

53

*Lettuce:* Round and Cos lettuce trimmings and thinned out plants may be fed. Little Gem is an easy variety to grow. We eat lettuces from sowings made out in the open garden in early spring right through to early winter. The rabbits have the outer leaves.

*Spinach:* An easy plant to grow at home. Choose an all the year round variety and leave the roots in the ground during the winter. New leaves will appear early the following spring. In a mild winter some growth of fresh foliage will be seen when little else is available.

*Fruit:* When there is a glut of fruit in the garden, rabbit-fanciers often feed a little to their stock, but this should be mainly in the form of tit-bits and introduced slowly. When they are used to fruit in the diet, rabbits can take a whole windfall apple a day (or even two if a large breed). However, always be careful what you feed to weaners and young rabbits — a few fresh apple peelings are usually relished with no ill effect. Other fruits may be given in small quantities, e.g. blackberries, gooseberries, pears, raspberries, strawberries, and wild strawberries. Young blackberry leaves will often tempt a rabbit when nothing else will, and they have a medicinal effect too.

### Quantities of food
Beginners tend to over-feed, while experienced rabbit-keepers have been known to under-feed. Of course, the ideal is to avoid these two extremes. Bearing in mind that there must be no sudden change, the following would be suitable for a medium-sized adults that is not carrying or feeding young: a cupful of rabbit pellets; a small bundle of hay (renewed daily); clean water. The pellets may be replaced by mixed cereals in similar quantities, or wholemeal bread and household left-overs as explained above.

### Do not feed
Remember, two home-grown vegetables that must not be fed are potato *leaves* and tomato *leaves* — the actual tomatoes are not likely to be fed to rabbits, but some rabbits seem to enjoy them in small doses. Cooked potatoes or potato peelings may be fed if mashed into bran or bread-crumbs. (The latter was a war-time economy feed.)

### Flowers that rabbits can eat
The following garden plants are not poisonous to rabbits and if you are having a tidy up, there is no harm in giving your rabbits a few tit-bits.

They like asters, calendula (English marigold), daisies, hollyhock, honesty, marguerites, Michaelmas daisies, nasturtium, roses, sunflowers and wallflowers. Young plants are always preferred to old ones. If your pet will eat the seeds of the giant annual sunflower, these may be saved and added to the winter diet.

## Plants poisonous to rabbits

It is best to avoid all bulbous plants as many are harmful to rabbits, e.g. bluebells, daffodils, hyacinths, snowdrops and tulips. Also avoid antirrhinum (snapdragons), arum, lily, anemone, buttercup, dahlia, delphinium, foxglove, gypsophilla, hellebore (Christmas rose), iris, laburnum, larkspur, lily of the valley, lobelia, love-in-the-mist, lupin seeds and poppy plants. Poisonous weeds include: celandine, deadly nightshade and hemlock. Some breeders consider bindweed or convolvulus as dangerous to stock — but against this view, in my experience, a handful of this plant has no ill effect when fed to healthy rabbits. However, it might be wise to give only a few leaves at first if your pets are not used to this weed.

## Straw as food

Where straw is used in place of hay, greens should also be given if possible. Straw is not suitable as a food for does in kindle or nursing, as a high-protein diet is required at that time — unless of course she is on a pellet ration and the straw is merely bedding at which she nibbles between times.

## Water

Fresh clean water is essential for all rabbits that are kept in captivity, whether they are on a diet of pellets or mixed foods. Occasionally one hears of owners who say they give no water to stock kept on an all-green diet. A rabbit raised entirely on generous quantities of young, juicy greens and roots may very well need no additional water — but a rabbit on a dry pellet or mixed diet with no drinking water, even for half a day, will be a sad creature indeed. It is vitally important to make regular checks of the water bottles. They may need filling twice a day in summer. Rabbits usually drink more water in summer than during the cold months. This is only to be expected as hot weather generally makes animals thirsty. It should be remembered that food cannot be digested without water, so a thirsty animal will not eat dry food.

A doe feeding young will always drink plenty of water. She needs to take in lots of liquid herself in order to make enough milk for the babies.

Fill up the doe's water container at every feed time during the day.

## Hygiene at feeding times

Attention to cleanliness helps towards success in any venture where human, animal or plant life is concerned. Whatever the chosen food, it should be fed clean and free from dust, dirt or mould. Wild food must be washed if it is thought that dogs could have run over the area. Garden greens must not be covered with soil, slugs or fungus. Hay is no good if it is mouldy.

Feeding pots and pans will need a thorough clean at frequent intervals. Tip husks out at every meal time. Water pots are best rinsed out each time they are filled. Make sure the bottom is not slimey. To avoid this give them a good wash under a hot tap every few days. Bottles need a scrub with a wire brush, otherwise a green colouration will occur on the inside.

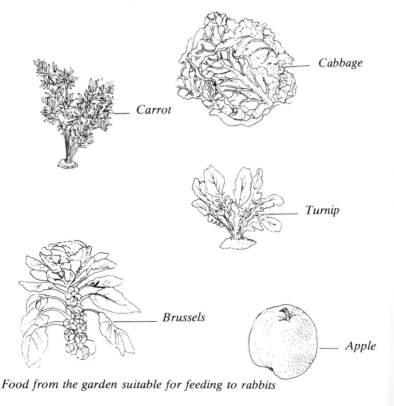

*Food from the garden suitable for feeding to rabbits*

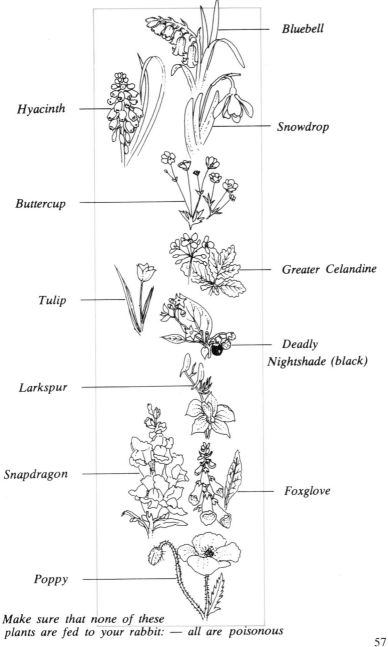

Bluebell

Hyacinth

Snowdrop

Buttercup

Greater Celandine

Tulip

Deadly
Nightshade (black)

Larkspur

Snapdragon

Foxglove

Poppy

*Make sure that none of these
plants are fed to your rabbit: — all are poisonous*

57

# Breeding

When you have owned a pet rabbit for several months or, better still, years, you will have gained a certain amount of experience. It is never a good idea to buy a doe especially for breeding if you have had no practical experience in the normal everyday management of young and adult rabbits. However, sooner or later, most people who own a pet rabbit feel it would be nice to have at least one litter of baby bunnies — and it is educational for the children.

Breeding rabbits can be a most enjoyable and inexpensive hobby, within the reach of nearly everyone, but as with almost anything worthwhile, a little knowledge of the subject is a great help. Contrary to popular opinion, rabbits do not always 'breed like rabbits'. Indeed, the comparatively new Netherland Dwarf breed can be quite slow to reproduce itself. A pair of mature adults have been known to spend the winter together without breeding at all! Yet another time, a doe might appear to accept the buck satisfactorily only to 'miss' and not give birth at the expected time. Also, many a litter is lost altogether due to freezing conditions.

A doe might do everything right: line her nest, place the babies neatly under cover, attend to them after birth, etc., and still lose the lot. Even in the late spring and summer — a good time for rabbit-breeding — Dwarfs give birth to small litters of between two and four kits, and it is only the knowledgeable breeder who will achieve success more often than failure.

If all this seems rather off-putting, it should be remembered that, generally speaking, rabbit-breeding is considered easy, and although some of the above troubles apply to all breeds — especially in the winter — even the novice should be able to gain a healthy litter of young rabbits.

The doe is perfectly capable of attending to the various stages of birth by herself; this is one reason why rabbit-breeding is a fairly simple procedure. Only very young does make mistakes, and this can be avoided by taking care not to mate maiden does before they are mature.

It is as well to bear in mind that although a litter of baby rabbits can be bred from any healthy pet-shop rabbit that is put to a buck — possibly another pet-shop rabbit — baby rabbits will be much easier to sell if they belong to a known breed. It is also far simpler to find homes for your surplus stock if they are pure-bred. Incidentally, it is useful to realize that many breeders who do not wish to make money out of their hobby do in fact charge a price for baby rabbits, simply to try to assure themselves that the babies are going to good homes. It is strange, but true, that something costing a few pounds or dollars will often be tended with more care than something that has been acquired for nothing.

The ideal is to begin with a healthy mature doe from a good breeding line. It is best to go to a breeder who specializes in the kind of rabbit that appeals to you. The secretary of the breed club will be pleased to put you in touch with someone who has surplus young stock to spare. It is advisable to purchase your doe when she is a youngster, not when she is in kindle. She will then have a chance to get to know you, and her new routine, before breeding begins. Most does that I have known took a long time to settle after a change when over the age of four months.

## The best age to mate

Some breeds mature at about twenty-four weeks; but the age at which a rabbit is ready for breeding varies with the breed. Some breeds mature at five months; others at around six months, the larger breeds tending to develop later than the small breeds. There are those who claim that healthy litters can be obtained by mating quite large breeds, such as the New Zealand White or the Californian, when they are only twenty weeks old, but these breeders are interested in raising cheap rabbits for the meat market. Owners of pet rabbits, or those breeding show rabbits, would do better to wait until a doe is older, say six to seven months old — eight and a half months if one of the largest breeds.

Once males are mature, they are able to mate at any time, providing they are in good condition. However, it is not often realized that animals can suffer psychological troubles which might prevent them from mating. A buck will sometimes refuse to mate when taken away from familiar surroundings; a young buck that has a bad experience with his first doe can prove difficult when required for future service — animals are more sensitive than is generally believed.

## Mating

The length of the female heat period is variable and the breeding season can be any time of year, although it is usually best in early spring. When the doe is stimulated, eggs are released from the ovary, but a fertile mating will not occur unless the doe is ready for the buck. As it can be tricky for the beginner to know when the doe is ready, the usual practice is to try her and then if she refuses the buck, try her again in six hours time. There should be little trouble experienced in getting a doe in kindle during a mild spring.

A question that often comes up is this: if a doe has a cross-bred litter, will her next litter be affected? The answer is that this is impossible. Each litter will only be the result of the buck used with the doe at the time of mating — poor bucks will leave no marks on future litters to a good buck.

To understand the above, it is necessary to know a little about what happens during mating. Briefly, the sperm from the male must reach the eggs of the doe for conception to occur. The sperm contains a number of microscopic chromosomes carrying genes, and these hold the pattern of inherited qualities that are in the male animal's breeding line. It is the same with the eggs from the doe. Thus a sperm meets with an egg inside the doe, and the combined pattern of genes forms the make-up of a new individual. The chromosome number must be suitable for a cross between two animals to be fertile, i.e., all *tame* rabbits are of one species with the same chromosome count.

The first step to be taken if you want a litter of rabbits is to introduce the doe to the buck. It is important to do it this way round. In other words, the buck is never put into the doe's hutch. It is essential to place the doe in with the buck. Some does are very possessive about their dwelling place. It doesn't always happen, but it is not worth taking an unnecessary risk.

Rabbits mate extremely quickly and a doe that is mature and in season will need no assistance. There will be a run round each other, a stamping of feet by either the doe or the buck, then the doe will stand still. The buck will mount the doe and within seconds fall off sideways, sometimes with a grunting kind of cry. That is all in a normal mating. Young does are often shy and quite frightened of the buck. They will aim to escape if possible, leaping for any gap in the cage or wire netting they can find, even to the extent of banging their heads against wood or other obstructions in their panic. Care needs to be taken.

Some breeders recommend holding a shy doe, or backing her into the buck's hutch. There may be some sense in the latter, but in my experience, the doe will only refuse the buck when already pregnant or having a false pregnancy, or if instinct (and hormones) tell her it is not a suitable time for mating to take place. For example, in late autumn or early winter, when the days are getting shorter, it is not unusual for the doe to try to escape the buck's attention. She will hop nimbly from corner to corner, sitting with her back to the sides of the hutch until the buck makes a move in her direction, when she will jump into the opposite corner. This instinct is sound: nine times out of ten, a month later it is freezing cold and any litter born would possibly die soon after birth.

The mating urge in rabbits is mostly due to instinct and hormone balance. It is nonsense to call a doe lazy if she will not accept the buck. Far better to obey nature and remove the reluctant doe from the buck's hutch. However, as already mentioned, during spring and early summer it is worth returning the doe to the buck about six hours later, as this second attempt — if not delayed too long — will often prove to be successful.

A doe that is ready for mating will often behave in a highly excited manner. She might hop up and down her cage, and perhaps stamp one of her hind legs. If very tame, a doe will throw herself on to her back at the touch of the owner's hand when being stroked, or more commonly she will raise the back part of the body. Although the upside-down position is not normal for mating rabbits, a young doe will sometimes roll on one side in an attempt to excite an old buck. A buck that has lived a celibate life for a number of years, as many a pet does, will often be rather slow to respond to the doe's mating behaviour. She may have to go as far as putting her foreleg round his neck or pulling mouthfuls of fur out of his neck in order to wake him up. In a similar way, a shy maiden doe usually responds to the attention of an experienced buck.

A word of warning about leaving bucks and does together too long: sometimes the two animals will not take to each other, and after a short time a fight might develop. This can even happen after a comparatively quiet mating or two. Suddenly the doe can turn and defend herself. Immediately the fur begins to fly and serious damage can occur in a short time.

After mating, carry the doe carefully back to her own hutch. Give her a bundle of clean hay and leave her to have a quiet munch. You could provide the buck with a handful of his favourite food too.

**Pregnancy**

Now you will have a pregnant rabbit to look after. The length of the gestation period in the rabbit is thirty-one days, so you can expect the litter a month after the day the mating took place. Make a note of the date the doe is due. If you have more than one doe, or several bucks, keep a record card with information such as name of sire, name of dam, mating date, expected kindling date, etc.

The female rabbit does not require much extra attention during the first two weeks of her pregnancy, so long as she is usually kept in good condition, fed and watered every day, and the hutch is cleaned out at least once a week.

About the end of the second week make sure the entire hutch has a scrub out. The rabbit is a clean animal and it will always endeavour to keep three-quarters of its hutch dry, soiling only one corner. Obviously, in time the entire floor would become wet and messy, but in a well-maintained rabbitry, one half of the hutch will be chosen by the animal as its sleeping place, and this will be kept dry for as long as possible. This is the side where you put extra bedding or a wooden box.

When cleaning out the hutch, from the third week of pregnancy onwards, only remove the droppings, wet straw, sawdust and/or news-paper from the soiled corner. Leave the nest-box with its contents of hay well alone. Make sure that there is plenty of bedding material in the hutch — especially from the twenty-fifth day onwards. There is no need actually to put it in the nest-box, as long as you place it on a dry area of the floor, and hopefully the whole of the hutch will be kept reasonably dry at this time. The doe will be quite happy to carry the bedding from one area to another in her mouth. She will build her own nest from the softest hay that you provide and from her own fur, which she plucks from the part of her body under her chin and down towards her abdomen.

It is often thought that if a doe builds a nest too early, she has probably been having a false pregnancy. However, against this view, I have known a doe to build a nest as early as the tenth day and still produce a litter at the right time. This was in the winter, and the doe was making her nest area thick with straw to keep herself warm during a frosty night, carrying large mouthfuls of yellow straw from one part of a large hutch to her bed. She did not line the nest with her fur, and this is probably a better clue to pseudo-pregnancy. If a doe lines her nest before the seventeenth day, it is possible to guess that the mating was not fertile.

Pseudo-pregnancy occurs sometimes when two does are kept together; when a buck is not fertile; or even when a maiden doe is housed next to a buck. In all these cases the eggs of the doe have not been fertilized, but the hormones react as if mating has taken place. The doe will build a nest and behave as though she is pregnant. The condition lasts for about eighteen days, and a doe is normally ready for mating again on the nine-teenth day. Therefore, if a mated doe has not increased her size round her middle by this date, some breeders like to return her to the buck. However, it can be difficult to tell if a rabbit is in kindle — even by the nineteenth day — and a pregnant doe should not be handled too much. Therefore, it is better for the beginner to wait until the thirty-first day and see if a litter is born. Let her run over her date by a day or two, as some does kindle as late as the thirty-third or thirty-fourth day, although this is less common. In most cases, no harm would come to the doe if she was re-mated when already pregnant, so long as she is handled gently. Many does refuse the buck when already in kindle. They sit in one corner making grunting noises and looking decidedly unhappy.

At the beginning of the third week after conception, give the doe nourishing food containing extra protein. For example, most pet does will enjoy a bowl of bread and milk at breakfast or supper time, in addition to a daily ration of pellets or cereal. When available, give your pet a handful of garden greens, clean grass or cabbage trimmings. She should have a large bottle or bowl of fresh water refilled daily — whether or not she has milk to drink.

**Birth**

The day before she is due to kindle, the doe will be less inclined to eat. She might eat nothing at all. This is quite normal during the twenty-four hours before birth begins, and for a short while after kindling. The mother rabbit will sit quietly and contentedly in the nest that she has made. She should not be disturbed, especially by children, cats, dogs, or people who are not known to her.

Make sure that a doe about to give birth has plenty of water within reach. It has been known for does kept short of water to kill their young.

The size of the litter will depend on hereditary patterns and on the number of eggs fertilized at the time of mating, plus the age of the doe: mature does tend to have larger litters than does older than three years, although a first litter is often smaller than average. Large breeds generally have more young per litter than small breeds. A rabbit can produce any number of young from one to thirteen, but six is about average — less for the Dwarf breed.

New-born rabbits are blind, deaf and without fur; quite dependent on the mother rabbit. They do not leave the nest for two to three weeks and their eyes remain closed for ten days.

It is a great mistake to keep interfering with the nest too soon after a doe has kindled. A doe will sometimes abandon her litter if she thinks her babies are being disturbed. In any case, it is best not to handle the young more than necessary. However, after twenty-four hours (four or five days if you are not experienced) you can carefully pull back some of the fur covering and peep inside just to see that all is well. Certainly, if there are one or two dead babies on the hutch floor, it is possible that the entire litter might be dead and an early inspection will be essential, but do not jump to conclusions too fast as sometimes in cold weather the kits can look dead when in fact they are alive. Occasionally a doe will put out just one dead body and the rest of her litter will be found warm and alive in the fur lining of the nest.

Some does are less fussy than others about someone well-known to them touching the nest. It is always the doe bought as an adult that gives the most trouble. This can be ascribed to nervousness. Give the doe some greenfood or a carrot to eat while you examine the nest. Do this as quickly as possible taking great care to cover the babies properly afterwards. Some breeders like to remove the doe from the hutch for a few minutes, but I have not found this necessary. In any case, be careful how you handle the doe at this time as her mammary glands will be full of milk. If you take her out for any reason, put her back as soon as possible. It cannot be stressed too strongly that the less you interfere with the nest the better, especially during the ten days after birth.

It is important to note that a good handful of hay should be given daily to the doe with a litter in the nest, otherwise she might eat the bedding hay that is needed to keep the babies warm. If given plenty of clean fresh hay every day, the doe will carefully arrange the right amount of covering over the nest, keeping more over the babies in cold weather and less in hot weather. The baby rabbits will also eat the hay in the nest as they get bigger, and begin to wean themselves before they leave the nest.

### Lactation

The female rabbit produces milk to feed her young for about seven weeks after kindling. During the first three weeks, the doe gives a lot of milk and it is very rich in nutrients. Therefore, she needs plenty of food. She will need around three times the quantity of her normal daily rations (presuming her every-day rations are adequate). This can be as much as two bowls of rabbit pellets and a large bowl of bread and milk, in addition to a generous helping of greenfood every day. (One half to a quarter of this will be enough for the Dwarf breed.) *Two* large bottles or bowls full of water will be necessary especially if the pet is kept largely on a pellet diet, as a lactating doe becomes thirsty at frequent intervals.

Baby rabbits grow very quickly on their mother's milk. The doe rabbit will give them all they need for the first three weeks, providing she is being given sufficient food and water herself.

Just before the third week, the youngsters will hop timidly out of the nest and using all four legs they will creep about rather than jump. If it happens before this time, it is possible that they are not receiving enough milk, which might indicate that the doe is not getting enough food and water. So the time the litter leaves the nest can serve as a rough guide to

*British Giant owned by
Mr. & Mrs. B. Adlard*

*Blue-eyed White Netherland
Dwarf owned by K. Beecroft*

*Harlequin doe at 10 weeks*

*Agouti Netherland Dwarfs:   A doe of good type (left) and a buck of
poor type (right). A little longer head is allowed in the doe*

*Lilac doe owned by Mr. A. Mort*

*Blue Beveren owned by H. Nicholson*

*An old pet buck—seven years of age*

management, although it is as well to take into account that very young does and very old does give less milk than a mature doe with, say, her second litter. Young does should give plenty of milk from the time their second litters are born until they are three years or slightly older. This does not mean that a doe will be unable to rear her first litter, or that an old doe will be unable to cope. However, a doe much over three years is considered old for breeding purposes.

## Weaning

When the baby rabbits are running about all over the hutch and nibbling at their mother's oats or pellets, or enjoying a small piece of bread, they are ready for weaning. Breeders who raise rabbits for the meat market say that it is possible to wean at three to four weeks old, but this is too early for the pet rabbits or show rabbits. You can *begin* to wean them at this time by placing a little bread or bread and milk in the hutch, but do not take the young rabbits away from the warmth of their mother until they are at least six weeks old. It will do them no harm if they stay with her for a further two weeks, but with some breeds a lot of large babies might begin to bother the doe after six weeks. It depends on the breed and the number of babies, and whether they are required for meat, pets, or show.

The doe likes to be left in her own home, so if possible remove the litter to another hutch when the time comes for the separation. Watch the feeding of the youngsters during the first week after they have been taken away from their mother, giving them slightly less greens than usual — certainly no large handfuls of white clover. Too much bulky greenfood at weaning time could result in bloat. However, the young rabbits will need as much cereal, pellets and/or wholemeal bread as they can eat until they are ten weeks old. After the first week or so of weaning, the greenfood can be increased gradually, as described in the chapter on feeding.

It is a good idea to feed three meals a day to newly weaned rabbits — if you can spare the time. Otherwise, feed them before you go to work and when you come home, at least until the babies are well-established. Some breeders always feed their stock twice a day, others give one good meal in the morning and a large handful of hay at night.

It is definitely a mistake to make two changes for rabbits on the same day if this can be avoided. For example, when removing the young kits from their mothers, do not change the type of water vessel, say, from a bottle to an earthenware pot on the same day if possible. Be careful to keep the food mixture exactly the same as you have been using for the previous few weeks. This rule applies to both the doe and the young.

## Fostering

If a doe dies, you may have to decide what to do with the baby rabbits. A number of breeders solve the problem by arranging to have more than one doe kindle at the same time, or within a couple of days of each other. The practice is not recommended unless a doe dies by accident, or unless she has too many babies of her own to feed (does have been known to raise litters of ten youngsters without mishap). It is easy to transfer disease from one lot of rabbits to another via one baby. In any case, this operation must be carried out before the kits are three to four days old.

If the doe knows you well she will be less likely to reject the new additions, but do not take any chances. It is wise to remove the receiving doe from her hutch while you place the babies from the other doe into her nest. Remember to handle the doe extremely carefully underneath, as if you bruise her she may get mastitis — a very painful infection of the milk glands. Let the babies mingle for a little while before putting the doe back, but not for so long that the babies become chilled.

Dutch and English breeds are considered to be the best for use as foster mothers, although a quiet-tempered doe of any breed may be tried.

## Hand-rearing

In the unlucky event of losing your only doe, you might wonder if it is at all possible to rear the babies by hand. The usual answer is that it is not worth the time and the effort. However, if you have plenty of time and, above all, patience, it is possible to raise a litter yourself, feeding the tiny babies on a mixture of two-parts cow's milk to one-part cool boiled water. First you will have to obtain a clean fountain-pen rubber lining and attach a section of tubing to this, as the little rabbits have very small mouths. Your chemist may be able to provide the rubber tube. Finally, the milk has to be given regularly at three-hour intervals through the day, and the kits must be kept warm on a covered hot water bottle. Always feed the milk warm, but it should not be too hot. You might be able to get the babies on to milk in a saucer by the time they are two and a half weeks old, and then you can slowly begin to add bread to the milk. It is easier to hand-rear baby rabbits in the summer than in the winter.

## Re-mating

A mature doe can give birth to several litters every year. If you are keeping rabbits as pets or for show, there is little point in breeding from a doe more than twice or, at most, three times a year. However, if necessary, you can safely put the doe back to the buck as soon as her litter has been weaned. She should give birth to another litter a month later. In the spring and early summer, this would do her no harm, although you might like to allow a longer rest in-between to let the doe build up her own strength.

Winter breeding is arranged by a number of rabbit-fanciers, but unless you have a properly built shed or the use of a light garage, mating between November and February is not recommended. Many litters in outdoor hutches are lost when the temperature drops below freezing. It helps if the hutches are given extra protection in bad weather, such as shutters, half-board fronts, overhead shelter, etc. Some litters are saved if the bedding is adequate, but even when every care is taken, baby rabbits are often lost during the coldest months.

Often the easiest time to get a doe in kindle is when the litter is between six and eight weeks old. One reason for this is that if a doe becomes too fat she is likely to be less fertile. However, it should be remembered that a doe in good condition makes a better mother than a worn-out thin rabbit.

### After weaning
When the time comes for the young rabbits to go to new homes, try to make sure they are wanted and that the prospective owner knows the basics of rabbit husbandry. Surely it is less cruel to kill them *if you know how to do this quickly and painlessly,* or have them humanely put down, rather than let them go to places where they might be treated badly or neglected. Owners of dogs and cats are usually quite fussy about demanding good homes for their puppies or kittens, but regretfully there is rather less concern over the disposal of spare baby rabbits. Perhaps the best remedy is found in not rearing more babies than are required. I know one breeder who has a waiting list, and she only mates her rabbits when she is sure she has people eager to buy all the youngsters. This method seems to work well.

### A look at genetics
The offspring that appear in a succession of litters from just one pair of rabbits can be surprising. For example, take a pair of Dwarfs. The sire was the wild agouti rabbit colour and the dam was chinchilla grey. Over two years they produced young in the following colours: black, white, agouti and chinchilla grey. Some litters contained all-grey rabbits; others contained two of one colour, two of another; and some, one black, one grey. There is further interest in this example: the agouti rabbit might breed true for that colour, or it might not. It depends on the genes the rabbit is carrying. The agouti rabbit could be carrying the genes for the

self rabbit (all-black, all-white, etc.).

This becomes even more interesting when we realize that there is a mathematical pattern in the way that the colours appear. There is sufficient knowledge of genetical principles to enable breeders to predict whether or not a particular colour could ever be obtained from a pair of rabbits before breeding begins.

Tame rabbits are beautiful animals, raised under careful conditions; but they have all been derived from wild ancestors. They have been bred in captivity over generations, and by selective breeding, individual characteristics such as short ears (as in Dwarfs), or enormous long ones (as in Lops), have been established.

Rabbit-breeders select a buck and a doe that exhibit the markings or body shape that they require in the offspring. It can be more complicated than this, as a rabbit may be carrying the genes for a characteristic that is not apparent in its physical appearance.

To begin at the beginning, each cell of the buck and each cell of the doe contain a number of pairs of chromosomes. Each hereditable characteristic is controlled by two genes — one on each chromosome of a pair. These genes control a wide range of characters: coat colour, shape of nose, type of ear, etc., and are arranged on the chromosomes like beads on a necklace. When reproductive cells are formed, egg cells in the doe and spermatozoads in the buck, one chromosome of each pair, and, therefore, one gene of each pair, passes into each reproductive cell. If a buck and doe breed true for, say, coat colour, it is probable that the two genes controlling coat colour are both the same in the buck and both the same in the doe — i.e. that all four genes are the same in the buck and doe. In this case, the animals are said to be *homozygous* for coat colour. (Animals having two different genes for the same characteristic are said to be *heterozygous* for that characteristic.) See diagram.

It is interesting to note that some genes are dominant to others — for example, the agouti wild rabbit colour (giving a soft-brown overall appearance) is dominant to the self-colour rabbit (all over one colour, i.e. black, blue, red, white, yellow, etc.). The self originally sported or mutated from the wild colour, and that is how other patterns have developed. However, as can be seen in the above example, a rabbit can be showing the dominant character while carrying a recessive character.

If two heterozygous parents are mated together, the progeny will be in the proportion of one homozygous agouti to two heterozygous agoutis to one homozygous self. In the example of Dwarf rabbits, the heterozygous rabbits were much more chinchilla-grey in appearance than the typical tan/black mixture of colours seen in the true agouti coat; but in other cases it is possible for the heterozygous agouti to look the same as the homozygous agouti. If one of the grey heterozygous rabbits is mated back to an all-white homozygous self, the offspring are in the proportion of one grey to one white. The homozygous rabbit will breed true; the heterozygous grey will have the same possibilities as its parent.

The required markings of the popular English rabbit are comparatively difficult to breed since the desired type is the heterozygous rabbit. In a litter, you get one Charlie (a rabbit with a Charlie Chaplin moustache!) to two English type to one self. Then, if you breed your English doe to an English buck, you obtain the same mixed litter again, and so on. Whereas, a Charlie crossed with a self gives you all-English babies in a litter. A Charlie crossed with another Charlie gives all Charlies, and self times self will result in all self.

The inheritance of the Himalayan coat colour pattern is interesting. A pink-eyed Himalayan Dwarf doe was mated to a brown-eyed grey Agouti Dwarf buck carrying genes for the albino character (i.e. pink-eyed white). Normally, the typical Himalayan breed markings of dark ears, nose, feet and tail on an otherwise white fur are dominant to the albino but recessive to every other colour. In this case, the doe gave birth to one brown-eyed off-white, two Agouti-type greys, and three quite well-marked Himalayan youngsters.

Presumably, where the genes for Agouti-grey met the genes for Himalayan pattern, the Agouti were dominant; but where the albino genes that the Agouti-grey buck was carrying met the genes for Himalayan coat of the doe, the Himalayan factor was dominant, as one would expect. The only unusual point being that both examples occurred in one litter. Dwarfs are inclined to produce very small litters of two or three young. Indeed, this doe had only two black kits in her next litter to a black Dwarf. They took after their father for type, being compact in body with round heads and bold eyes, and although black, they were both carrying the Himalayan factor (i.e. when mated together the white fur with colour-point markings reappeared).

Yet another fascinating example of genetics is seen in the rare Harlequin breed, where the best rabbits look rather like a cross between a chess-board and a bumble bee. On the question of genetics, self is dominant to the Harlequin pattern, but Agouti (wild colour) is dominant to self (all-over one shade). Therefore, any out-crossing (see below) to other breeds usually results in predominantly self or Agouti-type animals in the first generation, although the Harlequin pattern usually reappears in the second generation. In order to keep up the intriguing pattern, a well-marked Harlequin doe is mated to a well-marked Harlequin buck. It is quite a puzzle for the breeder to produce anything like a show specimen!

In addition to dominant or recessive genes, there are also *modifying* genes. Sometimes when two rabbits with contrasting characteristics are bred together, the offspring will show neither one nor the other, but something in-between, and the characteristic becomes more diluted with every generation. The blue coat colour in rabbits behaves like this.

The adult rabbit passes on to its offspring only one gene of each pair and as there are many different genes — length of hair, body size, width of head, shape of eye, etc. — each to be matched with one gene of a pair from the other parent, there is infinite variety for the pattern the genes will form during the conception of every new individual.

## In-breeding
This is a method of breeding that can be advantageous, but it is best avoided unless fully understood, as stock can quickly degenerate if similar faults are present in both sire and dam. The animals used for in-breeding are closely-related, e.g. mother and son, brother and sister, etc. It is a method that is sometimes used by rabbit-breeders who are trying to establish a good feature, as for example a bold eye or a deep colour. However a bad feature, such as difficult temperament or general weakness, can be bred in just as quickly. It is never a good plan to continue with in-breeding too long. Always bring in another buck or doe by at the latest the third generation.

## Line-breeding
The effects of this method are more gradual, but there are also less risks involved. Close relatives are mated together, but *not* brother to sister — even from two different litters of the same parents. It is usually grandson to grandmother, grandfather to grand-daughter, or cousin to cousin.

This system is often used by breeders wishing to build a strain of show-quality rabbits. If a particularly good buck is obtained which exhibits all the features of its type, then his best daughters might be bred back to him and later the best does of that litter will again be sent to him for service. Eventually, this is likely to lead to a number of the offspring showing good points similar to those of the original grandfather buck.

## Cross-breeding or out-crossing
This is the mating of a buck and a doe from different breeds. A practice not recommended to the owner of pet rabbits, as it is usually more difficult to find homes for the baby rabbits. However, all rabbits of the

domestic breeds belong to one species, *Oryctolague cuniculus,* and any healthy buck can be mated with any healthy doe to produce young — no matter what size, or shape, or colour, but it is not sensible to mate a large buck with a Dwarf doe. She might have trouble giving birth, although normally the doe bears young of a size she can manage.

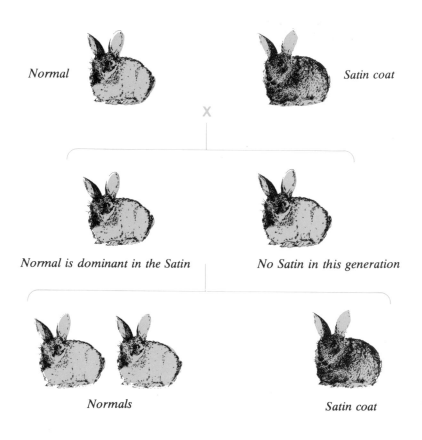

Normal

Satin coat

X

Normal is dominant in the Satin

No Satin in this generation

Normals

Satin coat

*The Satin coat is not necessarily a different COLOUR or a different LENGTH from the normal coat, but the special cell structure of each hair gives the fur a distinctive sheen.*

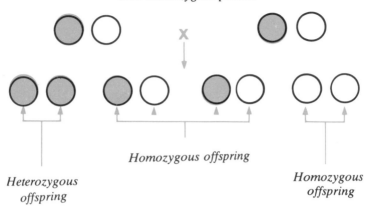

*Two heterozygous parents*

*Homozygous offspring*

*Heterozygous offspring*

*Homozygous offspring*

# Ailments

**Prevention**

Rabbits are healthy animals and if well-kept it is possible to avoid sickness completely. Many a pet bunny has lived its entire life-time of perhaps ten or more years without suffering from a single illness. However, it is advisable to know what do in in case of emergency. Accidents happen in the most unlikely places at the most unexpected times. You can help to prevent trouble by following a few basic rules:

1   Buy healthy stock from a reliable source.
2   Give sufficient food every day — many diseases begin from incorrect nutrition.
3   Provide plenty of fresh drinking water.
4   Allow a portion of hay per day to keep the digestion working steadily.
5   Never feed mouldy or frozen food.
6   Get to know which weeds and garden plants are poisonous.
7   Have hutches that are large with sufficient floor space for the breed.
8   Clean out hutches regularly to prevent disease from spreading.
9   Avoid getting your pet over-heated in the hot summer sun.
10  Remember that dampness is worse than cold for rabbits.
11  Watch for the first signs of illness, so that you can give early treatment, e.g. a runny nose or sneezing, scouring (loose droppings), a flesh wound, or a sore of some kind.
12  If you have several rabbits, always isolate a sick one.
13  Supervise children until they are old enough to understand how to be gentle and quiet with animals.
14  Lastly, two don'ts about cats and dogs — *do not* feed greens that have been overrun by these animals, and *do not* let other household pets frighten your rabbits, as stress can cause severe problems.

You can tell a healthy rabbit from its bright eyes, clean nose and well-fleshed body. This is the kind of pet that is attractive and a joy to own, but if your rabbit should look sick at any time, it should be possible to find a cure yourself for slight ailments, or in severe or chronic cases the local veterinary surgeon will be pleased to advise. Normally, where disease is concerned, the sooner you take your pet for treatment the better the chances of complete recovery. There will be little that the vet can do if an animal is already dying — besides putting it quickly out of its misery. Hopeless cases should be humanely put down.

Some of the simple ailments can be successfully treated at home. Many herbs and wild plants that grow in our hedgerows have curative powers. You can often bring a beloved pet through a nasty spot of trouble by gathering and feeding nothing but a special plant for a day or two. Blackberry leaves and growing tips of shoots have proved to be health-restoring when fed to my own rabbits over the years. Of course, part of the problem is getting to know which ailments need immediate attention by the vet and which ailments can be easily treated at home. Experience will teach you to make the correct decision, but in the meantime, if in doubt, contact your vet for his advice.

### Artificial respiration

This is difficult with adult rabbits, as even mouth to mouth breathing does not work. However, sometimes a youngster can be saved by moving its head downwards and then upwards very gently, slowly repeating the movements about two seconds apart. Stop as soon as the baby begins to breath. Then tuck it back into a warm nest or try the old country method of popping it down your shirt front for a few minutes. Warmth is needed to get the little body going. A rabbit-fancier, known to all Harlequin breeders, assures me that he put two babies in his trouser pocket while he ran round to his friend's house in order to make use of a foster doe. The babies were placed in the new nest and safely reared.

### Blows, blown, or hoven

There are several country names, including 'bloat', for a condition caused by pressure of gas from food, trapped in the animal's intestine. The rabbit suffers particularly badly from this complaint because it cannot bring up its wind like many other animals. Unfortunately, I had to learn about this illness the hard way. One of my first rabbits, a beautiful Ermine Rex, was given too much white clover after a long winter period on a diet that included few greens. The poor creature was found blown and too tight around the belly, its eye already beginning to glaze. I was a young child and there was nothing I could do except watch it go through all the stages of dying. The experience did teach me about the danger of giving lush green grass or juicy white clover early in the spring — for this is one of the ways a rabbit becomes blown — lots of leafy young greens after a spell on an almost dry diet. Always watch young rabbits the first time they are put out into a grass run, for example. Also underfeeding followed by overfeeding can cause bloat. However, a pet fed on a steady, well-balanced diet will probably never have this trouble.

*Treatment:* There is not a lot that can be done, and if the rabbit is already unwilling to move about, or already semi-conscious when found, it will be in great pain. Sometimes, a very small amount, say half a tea-spoonful, of medicinal Liquid Paraffin will move the obstruction and allow the gas to escape. This may be tried if the animal is not too far gone.

### Broken bones
Keeping rabbits permanently in a dark shed or building without sufficient light, in combination with a poor diet, can lead to brittle bones that easily become broken or fractured. Another cause is careless handling. Rabbits with broken bones are usually quickly culled by commercial breeders, but pets have been successfully cured by having their bones reset by a veterinary surgeon. I have heard of two cases where surgical plates have been necessary and there must be many others. (See also Injury and Rickets.)

### Canker
Hopefully you may never come across this pest, as it is not so common now as it was once. However, if your pet should keep on scratching behind its ears and then lick or chew the end of its toes, suspect canker and look to see if the ears are clean. A tiny mite *Psoroptes communis cuniculi* attacks the inside of the ear, causing intense irritation. The first signs that you will be likely to see are pinky-brown encrustations, or a wax substance. An infected animal might also shake its head and sit more quietly than usual in one corner.

*Treatment:* This is something that the vet can clear up quite quickly, especially if you follow his/her instructions carefully. Remember to clean out and disinfect the hutch, burning all bedding, as the mite can live for up to three weeks away from a host. If not destroyed they could reinfect the rabbit.

### Claws (overgrown)
Most owners dislike the thought of clipping their pet's nails. A rabbit's claws keep on growing and can be seen quite long and curled in an old

buck or doe. Wild rabbits wear their claws short by constant digging and running on hard surfaces. Pets sometimes need their claws clipped back at the tips, but do be careful not to cut into the quick. *Clipping claws too short is painful to the rabbit and they will bleed.* Only the dried horny tip of the nail should be cut. If in doubt, hold the nail up against the light, when you should be able to see the darker line of the quick inside. It is best to watch an experienced rabbit-keeper do the job the first time. If you do not think you could manage this, your vet would be able to help you.

Does used for breeding should have their claws clipped if they are very overgrown, otherwise the babies might be scratched accidentally. The doe usually tries to be careful when tending her young, but if she is disturbed and this causes her to move quickly, a baby's eye could be caught by mistake.

On an old rabbit the toe-nails will curl, and an experienced breeder can guess approximately the age of a rabbit by a glance at the claws.

*Clip your rabbit's nails if they become overgrown, but remember it can be painful if you cut them too short. Look into the nail against the light to see how far down the 'quick' goes.*

## Coccidiosis

This is a much-feared ailment in commercial rabbit units, so much so that it is often the number one excuse for keeping rabbits on wire floors. The eggs of the protozoa responsible for the sickness come out of a rabbit in the droppings and in a damp, warm corner of a hutch, the oocysts develop and reinfect the rabbit if picked up and eaten on food. The parasite then attacks the intestine or the liver. The intestinal species is called *Eimeria performa* or *E.magna* and the species which attacks the liver is *E.steida*. One way of helping to prevent coccidiosis is by keeping the hutch clean. Another way is to avoid over-crowding.

*Treatment:*  Contact your vet for advice if one or more of your pets dies for no obvious reason, or if youngsters fail to grow or put on any weight in spite of an adequate diet. Coccidiostats are available to cure cases that are not too far gone and there is a medicine that can be put into the drinking water to prevent the illness spreading to other rabbits.

## Chills

Baby rabbits can die from becoming too cold in the nest on an extremely cold night. Newly weaned youngsters taken separately to new homes sometimes catch pneumonia and die within a few hours from the double shock of changed environment and icy weather. So if you buy a new rabbit during winter, try to make sure that it has plenty of bedding material, such as hay or straw, and that the hutch provides adequate shelter from wind and driving snow. A rabbit can stand cold, but not whistling draughts or damp.

## Colds

Lack of ventilation or sunlight, and insufficient exercise can cause colds, but it is important not to confuse the common cold with the much more serious snuffles. The main difference from the pet-owner's point of view is that a cold will clear up within a week or two, whereas snuffles will not go away at all. Therefore, the best plan is to keep your rabbits well-fed in dry, draught-proof hutches in order to prevent illness. If you should be unlucky enough to spot a running nose on one of your pets, isolate it from other rabbits, and hope that the cold symptoms dry up within a few days. Do not immediately give it up as hopeless, as I have noticed that a doe with a young litter will sometimes develop a sniff which clears as the youngsters grow. *Never* buy a rabbit with a running nose, thinking that it is just a cold which will soon clear under your good management. The chances are that it will not. (See Snuffles.)

*Treatment:* Your vet can supply antibiotics to put in the rabbit's drinking water.

### Constipation
Sometimes known as *impaction,* constipation is caused by feeding only dry food and not enough water, hay and green plants, and it occurs occasionally when an animal licks too many loose hairs from its coat — especially if the diet is lacking in any way.

*Treatment:* Half a teaspoonful of castor oil or Liquid Paraffin (the medicinal kind). Dandelions will tempt the appetite and help the condition.

### Coprophagy
If you watch your pet rabbit closely for any length of time, you might observe what at first can appear to be a strange and, perhaps, disturbing habit. The rabbit eats some of its droppings. This is perfectly normal. The pellets are taken straight from the anus and not allowed to touch the floor. These pellets are different from the round, dark, straw-coloured droppings usually seen in one corner of the hutch. They are softer and contain part of the animal's food which hàs not been fully digested. Cows chew the cud twice and, in not quite the same way, some food goes through the rabbit's system a second time. This habit is very useful to the wild rabbit in times of harsh weather or danger above ground. However, it will be noticed by the observant that the normal faecal droppings are not eaten.

### Culling
This term is often used in rabbit circles. It means putting down an animal or animals that are incurably sick, or for other humane reasons. Of course, they should only be killed in ways that cause instant death and no pain. (See Mercy killing p.19.)

### Diarrhoea or scours
Enteritis or stomach upset can occur for a number of reasons including: a sudden change of diet and underfeeding followed by overfeeding — especially of wet greenstuff. Mouldy greens or frozen plants should also be avoided. Care needs to be taken with the diet of young rabbits. See that they do not fill themselves to capacity on wet grass. However, pet rabbits are not often troubled with diarrhoea if they are given food regularly and a diet that includes a bundle of clean hay every day.

*Treatment:* Minor upsets can be cured by feeding with young blackberry shoots, and bramble leaves with hay. At the same time, make sure the hutch is clean and comfortable. Bad cases, or cases where the enteritis is seen to be spreading to other rabbits should be seen by a vet. Medicine obtainable from the vet will act as a cure if the pet is not too far gone. *Remember the rabbit must have access to clean water even when scouring.*

## Fur chewing

This occurs from a deficiency in the diet or because the rabbit is bored. Hay or straw should be fed to provide the fibre that the rabbit's digestive system requires and also, strangely enough, to prevent boredom. A rabbit is usually quite happy if it has some nice clean hay to chew. You might catch your pet chewing the wood of the hutch — again this can be due to boredom or because of a need for more fibre. Feeding more hay will cure the habit.

## Heat exhaustion

If your pet should be accidentally exposed to the full heat of the summer sun with no shade for an hour or more, it will lie on its side breathing heavily. This might also occur if a rabbit has to spend time in a travelling box in a tent at a show, or in the back of a car on a hot afternoon. Obviously everything possible should be done to prevent these occasions from arising. Make sure there is some shade over the hutch in summer. A deckchair placed against a solitary hutch will serve as extra cover on an unusually hot day, but check to see that plenty of air can circulate underneath. Try to cool a rabbit suffering from heat as soon as possible.

*Treatment:* Provide clean cold water for the animal to drink and place it in a cool place such as a shady garage until recovery is observed. Sometimes a cloth rung out with cold water held against the rabbit's side has been found useful. All bedding should be removed until the rabbit shows signs of recovery, but take care to replace it as the rabbit cools down because you will not want your pet to catch cold.

## Injury

It is surprising how easily accidents happen, even when the greatest care is taken — and always when least expected. Therefore, it is as well to have a first-aid kit handy for your pets.

Fighting might be a source of trouble if more than one animal is kept in a hutch after the weaning period. However, youngsters may be run on together to the age of twelve weeks without much risk of damage.

Watch out for badly-designed or constructed hutches with loose sharp edges, feeding-pots that can turn into traps, or water vessels that can cause drowning to young weaners; and rabbits have been known to hang themselves in hay-nets.

Another common source of accidents is mishandling. Young children sometimes drop rabbits out of fright, so always supervise their early lessons in animal care and try to see that the first lesson on how to hold their pet takes place over soft ground, perhaps with someone ready to catch.

Torn claws are quite common, so place your pet slowly into its hutch or wire run. A rabbit will occasionally put out a paw and a claw is ripped out as it catches in the netting. This can seem quite alarming, as blood trickles out rather quickly. However, it is not so frightening as it appears.

*Treatment:* Fight wounds should be bathed with warm, diluted antiseptic solution. If they become septic, take your pet to the vet. Where torn claws are the case, wash gently with clean, warm water. You can put a bandage on if you wish, although most rabbits will have it off in an hour or two. The foot soon stops bleeding and nature takes care of the healing in a matter of days. Absolute cleanliness is essential where wounds are concerned. Clean the hutch every day if necessary.

### Insects

Flies and wasps are not wanted. Frequent cleaning is the best way to keep hutches free from fly larva, especially in summer. Sweeping up around the hutches also helps. Disinfecting the cages, or at least the rabbit's toilet corner, once a week during the hottest part of the year is advisable. Clear away all food that has not been eaten by the following meal time. Half-eaten fruit is particularly attractive to wasps and other stinging insects.

### Mastitis

When a doe knocks her mammary glands by, for example, getting in and out of a small nest-box, infection might set in. Or occasionally a bite from a baby on the nipple might become infected. There is also a danger of mastitis if a number of babies are removed from the doe and she produces much more milk than the remaining babies can take. In cases of infection, the area around one or more teats goes hard and becomes inflamed. I must stress that this is *most painful*. Do not press or massage. This will only make the illness worse.

*Treatment:* This is one of the ailments where it is worth calling in your veterinary surgeon or taking the rabbit to the animal clinic as soon as possible. In many cases, an antibiotic injection will be urgently needed if the pet is to be saved. Always handle a pregnant or nursing doe very gently. Avoid any kind of pressure on the mammary glands.

## Milk-fever

This is not just another name for mastitis, but an illness caused by mineral deficiency. One needs to step out one fine morning and come across a cow worth hundreds of pounds or dollars lying dead from a sudden lack of calcium, to appreciate this ailment fully. The calcium all goes into the milk, leaving the mother animal's body depleted. It can happen to a doe that gives birth to a very large litter of babies. Even when a pet has a great number of young, milk-fever rarely occurs when a good diet is given. This is simply because cows have been bred for generations to give enormous quantities of milk, whereas rabbits have only comparatively recently been selected for their milk-producing qualities. This form of selection is being practised on commercial rabbit farms nowadays and this is where milk-fever is more likely to appear.

*Treatment:* A mineral injection or food supplement supplied by the vet.

## Myxomatosis

This is another much feared disease among rabbit-keepers. Mr. R.M. Lockley writes vividly of his experiences regarding myxomatosis on the Island of Skokholm, which lies off Pembroke, in his book *The Island.*

It has been found that the virus is spread from one wild rabbit to another by fleas. Therefore, if myxomatosis is in your area, it might be worth having your pets vaccinated, as it is a gruesome sickness causing swelling of the eyelids and other parts of the head. Fortunately, most tame rabbits are free from fleas, which greatly lessens the chances of infection.

*Treatment:* Have the victim humanely put down as soon as myxomatosis is confirmed.

## Paralysis

This can be the result of continuous wrong feeding or confinement in a damp hutch.

*Treatment:* Mild cases may be placed into a dry hutch, where care and regular feeding with nourishing food might bring about an improvement within a few days. However, bad cases should be seen by a vet.

## Pneumonia
Very old and very young rabbits are the most susceptible to pneumonia. Babies in the nest subjected to exposure through lack of covering in extremely cold weather sometimes die overnight. An old buck or doe, eight years or more, might die suddenly, although pneumonia is often the final complication of some other illness. Does about to give birth are also vulnerable, especially when there is a dramatic change of temperature.

Among stock housed indoors the trouble usually arises on account of inadequate ventilation. Once again, attention to feeding and general care is the best way to prevent an outbreak. Pets in outdoor hutches that are properly protected against harsh weather are much less likely to develop pneumonia.

*Treatment:* Often not possible due to the rapid development of the illness. Penicillin injections might save a treasured pet if an early diagnosis is made.

## Poor appetite
A rabbit can go off its food for a number of reasons, and since a healthy animal always looks interested and eager at feeding times, lack of appetite should be taken as a warning signal. First consider whether you have been overfeeding your pet, or whether it is not long since you gave bunny a generous portion of some favourite tit-bit. Perhaps your pet is just not hungry. Next, take into account the weather. You should not expect a rabbit to eat much on a hot afternoon, unless it is near starvation. A rabbit's natural instinct is to lie about during the day and eat in the cool of the evening, especially in summer.

This said, if it is morning and if you have a youngster or a doe that is either pregnant or feeding a family, there is definitely something wrong if the pet will not eat (with the exception of the twenty-four hours before birth, when it is normal for a doe to go off her food). Young rabbits are usually prepared to eat at any time. Older animals and Dwarf rabbits are inclined to be pernickety over their food.

*Treatment:* If your pet has stopped eating completely, try to tempt with young green grass, tender blackberry leaves or raspberry leaves, shepherd's purse, dandelions, or willow leaves. Should these favourite plants be left untouched after some time, contact your vet as the lack of appetite could be a sympton of a more serious illness.

## Rickets

Some illnesses are caused through a deficiency of vitamins and/or minerals. Rickets is due to a lack of vitamin D which works with minerals, calcium and phosphorous to help make strong bones. Vitamin D is necessary for rabbit health as well as human health. It is known as the sunshine vitamin because it forms in the body when the skin is exposed to just the right amount of sunlight. Therefore rabbits should be housed in a place where they will receive some direct light every day although, of course, they should always be shaded from the hot mid-summer sun. Hutches are best situated facing south.

Animals that are so poorly fed that their diet lacks essential minerals may develop spontaneous bone fractures which lead to paralysis.

*Treatment:* Where a lack of minerals or vitamins is suspected, pets should be given plenty of greenfood and exercised in the open air in a grass run if possible.

## Ringworm

The rabbit kept simply as a pet seldom contracts this ailment, which is caused by a species of fungus. In any case, it is quite rare in the rabbit world.

*Treatment:* A pet should be taken to the vet for the latest preparation. Remember to wash your own hands thoroughly after attending to the rabbit.

## Running eyes

Breeds with large eyes are slightly more susceptible to eye trouble than breeds with smaller-sized or normal eyes. Where a wet patch down the fur round the inner corner of the eye is accompanied by a running nose and sneezing, then *Pasteurellosis* should be suspected (see Snuffles). However, running eyes without other symptoms can be caused by a draughty hutch.

Other eye disorders occur from time to time. For example, damage can be due to fighting; or a doe might accidentally catch the eye of one of her babies with a long claw when hopping over her litter, perhaps trying to avoid suckling during the daytime. In one case of this type, a well-marked four week old rabbit had an eye completely closed. The following day the eyelid was swollen and the area was sticky. The vet prescribed chloromycetin ointment, although he warned that it might not be possible to save the rabbit's sight in the eye. After four days of twice daily application the wounded eye was almost back to normal and the sight was saved.

*Treatment:*   Many cases of eye trouble will clear up rapidly if antibiotic ointment is prescribed. Rabbit-fanciers also favour Golden Eye ointment, which can be obtained from a chemist without prescription; but this should only be used for simple eye ailments. Once infection has set in, an antibiotic will be necessary. Always remember that a rabbit's eyes are most sensitive and treat them with care.

### Scurf
A form of dermatosis that is not ringworm. Symptoms include loss of fur around the face and ears; otherwise the rabbit appears to be normal. It is thought to be caused by feeding a diet that contains no greens.

*Treatment:*   Include some fresh grass and/or herbs in the daily diet.

### Snuffles
This is one of the worst illnesses of the rabbit — not because it is so severe or because it will necessarily kill the pet overnight, but because it is so difficult to cure.

Snuffles is the common name given to one of a group of diseases caused by *Pasteurella* bacteria. It is highly infectious and one rabbit quickly picks it up from another. It can also be passed on via a contaminated hutch, if a healthy rabbit is placed in a cage that has been recently occupied by one suffering from snuffles.

The illness has recognizable symptoms: the nose runs more or less continuously; the eyes run and there is a short dry sneeze. These are the early signs that can be easily recognized. During the ten to fourteen days while the animal is sickening for the disease, it is unusually lethargic, and the droppings might be more loose than usual. However, these last two early symptoms could be warning signs of other ailments. More certain is the running nose, for as the disease progresses, if left untreated, the mucus discharge becomes thick and yellow/white in appearance both from the nose and the eyes. The sneeze becomes more prolonged and a cough develops.

It is best to wait for the continuously running nose before deciding to cull the rabbit, if that is your intention.

Some say that snuffles (the organism *Pasteurella)* only flares up when adverse conditions for the rabbit are present. However, pet rabbits are extraordinarily healthy as a rule, and they will stand extremely cold weather without going sick. They can live out their entire lives without ever having the slightest symptom of snuffles. The disease has to be present in the vicinity for the rabbit to show symptoms.

*Treatment:* You may be wondering whether it is worth keeping a rabbit if by some unlucky. chance your pet picks the illness up from another rabbit — the decision will be up to you. It may be worth trying to save one beloved family pet. There *is* a cure, but it is not always successful: about 20 per cent of sick rabbits will not respond at all to the treatment, and even among those that show signs of improvement many will succumb at a later date. Breeders certainly advise culling as soon as the disease is confirmed. It can be heart-breaking to spend months tending a sick rabbit only to see it die in the end. It is worse for the breeder, as six months later the litter might perish and so on.

To cure a pet an antibiotic is necessary. The vet might prescribe oxytetracycline, which is administered either by injection or as a powder to mix in with the rabbit's drinking water. The mixture is replaced with fresh medicine every day.

**Sores**
Sores on the back feet seem to be too common and Rex rabbits have been found especially prone to ulceration in this region due to their short fur. The first thing to do is find the cause. Wire cages frequently prove to be the cause of this trouble. Pet rabbits are less likely to have this ailment, as they are usually kept in hutches with solid floors.

*Treatment:* Change to a wooden floor or place a large square of wood on a wire floor, so that the rabbit can rest comfortably. If possible, allow the invalid to run on clean grass every day. Penicillin injections will be found effective in cases where the sores have become infected. Less serious cases may be helped by bathing with clean, warm water. After gently drying (remember these sores are extremely painful) apply zinc and castor-oil cream. Of course it is important to keep the bedding dry and clean.

**Travel sickness**
Rabbits cannot be sick like many other animals, therefore they show their discomfort in other ways, for example, by going right off their food even when a journey is over. Make sure sufficient air can get to animals that have to travel for any reason.

*Treatment:* When a pet has been on a car journey and it is off its food, provide clean cool water and leave it in a *quiet* place to recover. Some herbs or fresh grass might tempt the appetite.

**Torticollis**
You might also hear this illness referred to as 'Twisted neck' or 'Wry neck'. The poor animal suffering from this ailment holds its head bent to one side. It often results from neglect of some other disease, such as ear canker.

*Treatment:* Immediate attention to ear canker (if found to be present) might save the rabbit, but advanced cases should be humanely put down.

**Vent disease**
There are at least two different kinds of vent disease and so it is as well to determine the cause before seeking treatment. A vet should be consulted if the cause remains obscure.

The contagious type is a venereal disease of rabbits passed from one animal to another during mating. It is caused by an organism called *Treponema cuniculi.* (Rabbit venereal disease is not transmitted to man.) You should suspect this illness if your pet becomes bare in the area around the sexual organs. Ulcers will follow and these will become covered with scabs.

However, pet rabbits are unlikely to contract vent disease; although care should be taken when purchasing fresh stock or sending a rabbit away for mating.

The buck with vent disease will probably refuse to mate, but his general condition will not deteriorate too rapidly for treatment. Does can also be affected.

*Treatment:* Make sure feeding and housing are up to standard. The vet will be able to prescribe an antibiotic that clears the disease up quite quickly if the instructions are followed carefully.

**N.B.**
Urine burn can look similar to venereal disease and it is also referred to as vent disease by many rabbit-fanciers. However, clean cage conditions will prevent urine burn, which is caused by wet bedding or a hutch containing a build-up of wet manure and little or no litter. Once sores have become contaminated with bacteria an antibiotic might be needed to clear the infection.

## Wounds

Deep gashes obtained in a fight with another rabbit or from an encounter with a cat or a dog should be seen by a vet, as stitches may be necessary. Unless the victim is a dearly beloved pet, it is sometimes advisable to have a badly wounded animal painlessly killed. The treatment for nasty accidents can be long and expensive.

Cats have been known to bite the limbs off baby rabbits and foxes will do the same to mature does, so take care to see that your pets are well protected.

## Worms

Fortunately, pet rabbits are not very prone to parasitic worms. If your pets are comfortably fed and housed, you will probably never come across this problem in your rabbits. One of the ways that rabbits can pick up parasitic pests is by eating plants that have been fouled by dogs suffering from worms. Therefore some caution regarding the selection of wild greens and grasses that you gather for your pets is advised. Growing your own rabbit food is a good idea, or pick greenery from suitable wild plants that grow beyond the reach of dogs.

Rabbits are not affected much by round-worms. There is a special caecal worm that you might come across, but pets do not usually suffer from them. Tapeworms are more serious. The eggs are picked up from the faeces of cats or dogs. These develop into cysts which can occasionally be felt under the skin of an infected rabbit.

*Treatment:* There are various country remedies for round-worms, amongst which garlic is said to be a good preventative if fed to stock. A suspected case of tapeworm should be seen by the vet. Confirmed victims are best humanely put down. Remember, never feed carcasses to dogs or other carnivorous animals as the parasite is passed on to another host in this way.

## First-aid for human attendants

Even a tiny scratch should be treated immediately with an antiseptic cream or lotion after washing. Rabbits are normally docile animals, but they often scratch unintentionally when frightened, so have a tube of antiseptic cream always handy. Wash your hand, dab it dry with a clean towel and apply the medication immediately to prevent infection.

## First-aid box for rabbits

Antiseptic cream or lotion.

Bottle of disinfectant.

Cotton wool.

Golden Eye Ointment.

Pair of scissors.

Pair of tweezers.

Small bottle of liquid paraffin or olive oil for constipation.

Small bandage.

Vaseline or zinc and castor-oil to prevent soreness.

It is worth repeating that cleaning hutches once or twice a week and feeding regularly every day will go a long way towards preventing ailments. Rabbits are pretty healthy animals and many a pet has passed a life-time without suffering any severe illness.

# Showing

Rabbit shows are held all over Britain and America. Many of the local shows are advertised in the journals devoted to small livestock and entry forms are available upon application to the club secretaries. In Britain, the best guide to what is happening in the rabbit world is the weekly journal *Fur and Feather*.

All show-rabbits in Britain are rung, that is, they wear a British Rabbit Council ring on one of their hind legs. These rings are slipped into place when the rabbits are six to eight weeks old. If the correct ring size for the breed is used, little or no discomfort seems to be experienced (although very occasionally a ring has been seen to have rubbed a little on a rabbit in generally poor health). Normally, the ring appears to be as unobtrusive as a wedding ring. Once the ring has been put on, it will be impossible to remove it from a live rabbit after a week or two has passed. This is advantageous to the breeder or showman as it serves as a permanent identification, due to the individual number on the ring. The British Rabbit Council keeps a complete record of all the numbers and owners. In addition, the year the ring was purchased is engraved on it and this is a rough record of the rabbit's age, i.e. to the nearest year.

If you intend to show one of your pets, first make sure you are quite familiar with the Standard for your particular breed. There is no reason why a rabbit of show standard should not be kept as a pet. You might even be lucky enough to breed a winner yourself if you try to obtain a pet from first-class stock when you make your initial purchase.

The next step is to join the National Club for your chosen breed. Most likely you will receive a Year Book, which will include a lot of useful information regarding the finer points of the breed and some news from other fanciers along with details about their champions. There should also be dates of shows and meetings in the current year.

Alternatively, you might join your local rabbit club and enter your pet in some of the classes at one of the shows, which will probably be held within easy travelling distance from your home. You will then meet other keen fanciers and they will be pleased to help you progress from there.

Rabbit enthusiasts are usually very friendly people. You will hear snippets of conversation about the merits of roll-back or fly-back coats; the advantages or disadvantages of various feeding methods; and most of all about the wonderful youngsters that are 'running about' in the latest litters.

However, in the first instance, you might prefer to visit a show without actually entering your rabbit. A large national show is a spectacular event with hundreds of rabbits on exhibition. Fortunately, most owners prepare their exhibits so well that they do not seem frightened of all the movement and noise. They sit quite still on the show-bench and rarely struggle when the judge handles them with expertise.

Most club members are not competing for prize money so much as for points, certificates and trophies. The hope for many is to obtain a championship award. A champion is usually a splendid animal whatever its breed. To see a champion of your own breed gives an idea of what to look for in the nest. In some breeds it is possible to spot a future champion when the baby is only a few days old. Youngsters of other breeds must be several weeks or months old before true potential can be fairly assessed. In the Dwarf breed, for example, a kitten of two weeks can be spotted as true-to-type in the nest, but the rabbit will be eighteen months before its full beauty is obvious. The head and eyes develop and change as the months pass. At about six months the youngster will be looking pretty good if it is suitable for showing.

The National Breed Clubs set the Standards according to which the rabbits are judged. Every week thousands of rabbit-fanciers take part in local shows. In addition there are numerous breed clubs which specialize in shows for one type of rabbit. In these shows many different varieties and colours of one breed can be seen and compared. The highlights of the year for the rabbit-owner with a champion or near champion are the two big events: the London Championship Show in October and the Bradford at Doncaster in January.

**Travelling to a show**
A small local show is a one day affair and rabbits are usually taken to and from the regular venue by car. The show-rabbit in tip-top condition is placed in a special wooden container, known as the travelling-box. This is trunk-like in appearance, sometimes containing two or more compartments to take more than one rabbit. It is most important that the box should be properly designed to allow enough ventilation. Several good boxes are offered for sale in the livestock press, but many fanciers make boxes themselves to suit their own special requirements, size of

breed, etc. A little hay is placed in the box with the rabbit unless it is an Angora or other long-haired breed, when the hay might become tangled in the coat. Sometimes a small crust is added for comfort.

Any pet-owner who intends to take part in shows will, sooner or later, develop an interest in producing a winner. It is certainly true of rabbits that a winner is a born winner. The qualities needed are produced by careful breeding; although this does not mean that a promising youngster will necessarily win as it might be spoilt by a bad environment. Careful feeding, housing and attention to detail in daily management all help towards producing a champion.

# Useful Addresses

British International Standard Rabbit Club — Miss Meg Brown, 24 Park Grove, Cardross, Dunbarton, Scotland.
British Rabbit Council, Purefoy House, Newark, Notts, England.
Commercial Rabbit Association, Tyning House, Shurdington, Cheltenham, Glos., England.
National Young Fanciers Society — Mr. K. Bee, 79 Boundary Road, Newark, Notts., England.

**Hutches and equipment**
Park Lines & Co., 501 Green Lanes, London, N13 4BS, England.
C.A. Sydenham Hannaford, Hamworthy Junction, Poole, Dorset, England.

# Bibliography

*Fur & Feather* — (U.K. weekly journal), Idle, Bradford, West Yorkshire, BD10 8NL, England.
*The Domestic Rabbit* — J.C. Sandford, pub. Crosby Lockwood 1969.
*Book of the Netherland Dwarf* — D. Cumpsty, pub. Spur Publication 1978.
*The Private Life of the Rabbit* — R.M. Lockley, pub. Deutsch 1965.
*The Island* — R.M. Lockley, pub. Deutsch 1969.

# Index

vitamin deficiency, 83

Water, importance of, 55–6, 63
water bowls, 41–3
weaning, 65
weights of rabbits, ideal, 6

worms, 83, 87
wounds, 79–80, 87
'wry neck', 86

Young rabbits, care of, 63–7